menu
plan eat enjoy

SIMON & SCHUSTER
A CBS COMPANY

Kim Morphew

First published in Great Britain by
Simon & Schuster UK Ltd, 2007
A CBS Company
Copyright © 2007, Weight Watchers International, Inc.
Simon & Schuster UK Ltd, Africa House,
64–78 Kingsway, London WC2B 6AH
This book is copyright under the
Berne Convention.
No reproduction without permission.
All rights reserved.

Weight Watchers, *POINTS* and **Core Plan** are trademarks of
Weight Watchers International, Inc., and are used under its control by
Weight Watchers (UK) Ltd.

Weight Watchers Publications Team
Jane Griffiths, Donna Watts, Nina Bhogal and Nina McKerlie
Photography by Steve Baxter
Styling by Rachel Jukes
Food preparation and styling by Penny Stephens
Design and typesetting by Jane Humphrey
Printed and bound in China

A CIP catalogue for this book is available from the British Library

Pictured on the front cover, from left to right: Full English bake page 11,
Cheat's soup page 18, Black Forest trifle page 84.
Pictured on the back cover, from left to right: Salmon strudel page 68,
Strawberry cheesecake page 46.

 POINTS® value logo: You'll find this easy to read *POINTS* value logo on every recipe throughout this book. The logo represents the number of *POINTS* values per serving each recipe contains. The easy to use *POINTS* **Plan** is designed to help you eat what you want, when you want – as long as you stay within your daily *POINTS* allowance – giving you the freedom to enjoy the food you love.

You'll find this distinctive **Core Plan**™ logo on every recipe that can be followed freely on the **Core Plan**. These recipes contain only foods that form part of the **Core Plan**.

This symbol denotes a vegetarian recipe and assumes that, where relevant, organic eggs, vegetarian cheese, vegetarian virtually fat free fromage frais and vegetarian low fat crème fraîche are used. Virtually fat free fromage frais and low fat crème fraîche may contain traces of gelatine so they are not always vegetarian. Please check the labels.

This symbol denotes a dish that can be frozen.

Recipe notes

Egg size: Medium, unless otherwise stated.

All fruits and vegetables: Medium sized unless otherwise stated.

Raw eggs: Only the freshest eggs should be used. Pregnant women, the elderly and children should avoid recipes with eggs which are not fully cooked or raw.

Recipe timings: Are approximate and meant to be guidelines. Please note that the preparation time includes all the steps up to and following the main cooking time(s).

Polyunsaturated margarine: Use brands such as Flora Light, St Ivel Gold, Benecol Light and Tesco Healthy Living Olive spread.

Rice: If following the **Core Plan** remember to use brown rice. If using white rice, remember to calculate the *POINTS* values.

Core Plan: If following the **Core Plan** you have a limited allowance of 2 teaspoons of healthy oil a day (olive, sunflower, safflower, flaxseed, rapeseed) to use in recipes as you choose.

contents

introduction

The Weight Watchers programme offers two food plans to help you to eat wisely and lose weight: the **POINTS Plan** and the **Core Plan**. *menu plan eat enjoy* has been designed to make life easier for you by giving you delicious and straightforward menus and quick, simple to follow recipes.

If you're following the **POINTS Plan**, we've allocated 18 **POINTS** values in total for breakfast, lunch, dinner and dessert and 2 **POINTS** values for your daily pint of skimmed milk. You can adjust the portion sizes if you have a daily **POINTS** allowance higher or lower than 20.

Core Plan menu plans are made up of three nutritious meals a day, and you can eat as much as you need to feel satisfied. Between meals, limit snacks to fresh fruit and vegetables and Weight Watchers Fruities. You also have an optional weekly **POINTS** allowance of 21 to spend either on foods that aren't on the Core Food List, or on Core foods that you want to eat in between meals.

The menu plans and the recipes in *menu plan eat enjoy* include one pint of skimmed milk (or its equivalent) each day to keep your calcium intake at the recommended level. You can use the milk in coffee, tea or as a drink on its own as well as in meals. If you're having cereal, the milk should be taken from your allowance or if your meal includes low fat plain yogurt (100 g), reduce your milk intake to $1/2$ a pint.

Chocolate torte, page 82

the Core Plan
menu plans

On the **Core Plan** you control calories by focusing your eating on a list of **wholesome, nutritious foods without tracking**. All the recipes and menu plans in this chapter will give you some inspiring ways to use the foods on the **Core Plan list**, making this food plan **simple and easy** to follow.

Full English bake, page 11

Weekend fry up

Breakfast **The ultimate hash browns:** (see recipe) served with grilled tomatoes. A kiwi. A pot of low fat plain fromage frais. A latte made with hot skimmed milk from your daily allowance, whizzed with a frother and mixed with 1 tsp instant coffee.

Lunch **Chicken salad:** mix bite size pieces of skinless roast chicken with chopped beef tomato, sliced celery stick, diced green pepper and a handful of mixed salad leaves. Drizzle over 1 tbsp low fat plain yogurt mixed with 1 tsp mint sauce and 50 g (1³/₄ oz) grated cucumber. An apple.

Dinner **Riviera pasta:** cook dried spaghetti according to the packet instructions. Meanwhile, gently heat 125 ml (4 fl oz) passata, 1 tsp extra virgin olive oil, low fat garlic and herb soft cheese, chopped ham, halved cherry tomatoes, sliced black olives and 1 tsp herbes de Provence. Drain the pasta and toss with 1 tsp extra virgin olive oil. Add the tomato sauce and season.

Ⓥ *Dessert* **Iced tea fruit:** infuse 1 tea bag in 100 ml (3¹/₂ fl oz) boiling water for 3 minutes. Remove the teabag and add 6 ice cubes and 100 ml (3¹/₂ fl oz) chilled diet lemonade. Put 1 cored, thinly sliced apple, 75 g (2³/₄ oz) hulled, sliced strawberries and a few mint sprigs into a bowl. Pour over the iced tea and chill until required. Serve with 1 tbsp low fat plain fromage frais.

Calcium guidelines Add 150 ml (5 fl oz) skimmed milk to this menu plan to keep your daily calcium intake at the recommended levels (see p. 80 of your Eat Wisely book).

The ultimate hash browns
Takes 30 minutes *Serves 4*

14 POINTS *values per recipe*
215 calories *per serving*

low fat cooking spray
3 rashers of lean back bacon *chopped roughly*
275 g (9¹/₂ oz) cooked green vegetables *such as leeks and broccoli*
400 g (14 oz) boiled potatoes *mashed*
1 teaspoon Dijon mustard
1 teaspoon wholegrain mustard
1 tablespoon white wine vinegar
4 eggs
salt and freshly ground black pepper

❶ Heat a non stick frying pan and spray with low fat cooking spray. Gently cook the bacon for 5 minutes until crispy. Remove and drain on kitchen paper.

❷ Roughly chop the green vegetables and put into a large bowl. Add the mashed potato, mustards and cooked bacon. Season and mix together.

❸ Using wet hands, divide the mixture into four and then shape each quarter into a large patty or burger shape.

❹ Heat the frying pan you cooked the bacon in and spray again with low fat cooking spray. Gently fry the potato cakes for 10 minutes, turning once (do not attempt to turn until after 5 minutes). Once cooked, transfer to a plate and keep warm.

❺ Meanwhile, bring a pan of water to the boil. Add vinegar to help make the perfect eggs. Crack in four eggs and poach for 5 minutes until opaque. Remove with a slotted spoon and place on top of the hash browns. Season with freshly ground black pepper and serve.

Ⓥ **Vegetarian tip:** replace the bacon rashers with three Quorn style bacon rashers and cook according to packet instructions, for a **POINTS** value of 2¹/₂ per serving.

Raspberry and banana muffins

Takes 10 minutes to prepare + 30 minutes cooling, 30 minutes to bake

Makes 6

14 POINTS *values per recipe*

165 calories *per serving*

250 ml (9 fl oz) skimmed milk

150 g (5^1/$_2$ oz) semolina

1 small banana *mashed*

3 eggs

zest of 1 lemon

3 tablespoons granulated artificial sweetener

^{1}/$_2$ teaspoon bicarbonate of soda

75 g (2^3/$_4$ oz) fresh raspberries

① Preheat the oven to Gas Mark 4/180°C/fan oven 160°C and line a six hole muffin tin with muffin cases. Heat the milk and semolina in a saucepan, stirring until really thick. Leave to cool completely (about 30 minutes) and then cut into small pieces.

② Whiz the banana and cooked semolina pieces in a food processor until smooth. Add the eggs, lemon zest, sweetener and bicarbonate of soda. Whiz again until smooth.

③ Empty into a bowl and fold through nearly all of the raspberries. Divide the mixture between the muffin cases, top each with a few raspberries and bake in the oven for 25–30 minutes until golden and risen.

Note: on the **Core Plan** these can be eaten only as part of a meal.

A good start

Ⓨ *Breakfast* **Raspberry and banana muffin:** (see recipe). A pot of fromage frais.

Ⓨ *Lunch* **Butternut squash soup:** simmer 150 g (5^1/$_2$ oz) cubed butternut squash, 200 ml (7 fl oz) vegetable stock, a pinch of ground ginger and the zest of an orange for 15–20 minutes. Whiz in a blender until smooth and season. Wholewheat crispbreads. An orange.

Ⓨ *Dinner* **Stuffed peppers:** mix 125 g (4^1/$_2$ oz) cooked brown rice, 50 g (1^3/$_4$ oz) chopped, blanched asparagus spears, 1 tbsp chopped fresh coriander, 2 tbsp low fat garlic and herb soft cheese. Season. Fill a red pepper with the rice mixture. Drizzle over 2 tsp olive oil. Bake at 190°C for 20 minutes. Serve with a salad.

Ⓨ *Dessert* **Berry ripple ice cream:** purée 75 g (2^3/$_4$ oz) strawberries with 1 tsp artificial sweetener. Mix together 1 tbsp low fat soft cheese with 150 g (5^1/$_2$ oz) low fat fromage frais until smooth. Put into a small freezable container. Pour over the strawberry purée. Freeze for 2 hours, stirring with a fork after 1 hour to marble.

Full English bake

Takes 30 minutes *Serves 2*

8¹/₂ *POINTS* *values per recipe*
190 calories *per serving*

4 rashers of lean back bacon
1 small red onion *cut into thin wedges*
low fat cooking spray
10 cherry tomatoes on the vine *cut into 2 separate vines*
75 g (2³/₄ oz) breakfast mushrooms (small field mushrooms)
1 tablespoon dried mixed herbs
200 g can of reduced sugar and salt baked beans
salt and freshly ground black pepper

1 Preheat the oven to Gas Mark 5/190°C/fan oven 170°C. Put the bacon rashers and onions in an ovenproof dish, spray with low fat cooking spray and bake in the oven for 10 minutes.

2 Add the tomatoes and season. Scatter around the mushrooms and sprinkle with the dried herbs, ensuring everything is evenly arranged. Spray again with low fat cooking spray and cook for a further 10 minutes.

3 Add the baked beans, filling in the gaps of the dish and cook for a final 5 minutes. Season to taste and serve.

Ⓨ Vegetarian tip: use four Quorn style bacon rashers instead of the lean back bacon, for a ***POINTS*** value of 2 per serving.

English breakfast

Breakfast **Full English bake:** (see recipe) with a large cappuccino made with hot skimmed milk from your daily allowance, whipped with a milk frother or whisked until foamy and added to strong coffee or espresso.

Lunch **Garlic chicken:** cooked skinless boneless chicken breast tossed with diced baby beetroot, radish, and lamb's lettuce and drizzled with fat free garlic and herb style dressing. Wholewheat crispbreads spread with low fat chive and onion soft cheese. A banana.

Dinner **Roast lamb:** a slice of roast lean lamb leg, served with diced sweet potatoes, drizzled with 2 tsp olive oil and cooked in a preheated oven at 190°C until crispy. Serve with cauliflower, broccoli and carrots.

Ⓨ *Dessert* A pot of low fat fruit fromage frais and a bowl of fresh cherries.

Calcium guidelines Add 150 ml (5 fl oz) skimmed milk to this menu plan to keep your daily calcium intake at the recommended levels (see p. 80 of your Eat Wisely book).

Feast of flavours

(Y) *Breakfast* A medium bowl of non sugary cereal with skimmed milk. $^1/_2$ a grapefruit.

Lunch **Artichoke and chicken salad:** (see recipe). A pot of low fat fruit fromage frais.

Dinner **Chilli potato wedges:** spray scrubbed sweet potato with low fat cooking spray, cut into wedges and bake in a preheated oven at 190°C for 45 minutes. Meanwhile, gently cook $^1/_2$ a small, finely chopped onion and 1 crushed garlic clove in a non stick pan with 2 tsp olive oil for 3–4 minutes until softened. Add extra lean beef mince and brown in the pan for 5 minutes. Add 6 tbsp passata, 2 tbsp water, 1 tsp Worcestershire sauce, $^1/_2$ tsp chilli powder and a 200 g can of drained and rinsed kidney beans. Cover and simmer for 20 minutes. Serve with the potato wedges and a salad made of avocado slices and 1 tbsp 0% fat Greek yogurt.

(Y) *Dessert* **Baked bananas:** cut a banana in half and sprinkle with a little freshly grated nutmeg. Sandwich the banana back together, wrap in foil and bake in a preheated oven at 190°C for 10 minutes. Serve with 1 tbsp low fat plain fromage frais.

Artichoke and chicken salad

Takes 30 minutes *Serves 2*

2$^1/_2$ POINTS *values per recipe*
170 calories *per serving*

1 small red onion *cut into thin wedges*
low fat cooking spray
4 baby courgettes *trimmed and halved lengthways*
1 x 400 g can of artichoke hearts in brine *drained and halved*
1 tablespoon capers *rinsed well*
2 tablespoons chopped fresh flat leaf parsley
25 g (1 oz) mild pepperdew peppers *drained and sliced finely*
100 g (3$^1/_2$ oz) skinless thinly sliced cooked chicken
4 tablespoons balsamic vinegar
salt and freshly ground black pepper

① Put the onion in a bowl and spray with low fat cooking spray. Heat a griddle or non stick frying pan until hot and cook the onion wedges for 3 minutes. Put the courgettes and artichoke hearts in the bowl and spray with low fat cooking spray.

② Turn the onions over and add the courgettes and artichoke hearts. Cook for a further 5–8 minutes until chargrilled and tender, turning halfway.

③ Meanwhile, put the capers, parsley and peppers into a bowl. Add the chargrilled vegetables and gently toss to combine. Season. Divide the chicken slices between plates and top each with half the warm chargrilled vegetables.

④ While the griddle or non stick frying pan is still warm, add the balsamic vinegar to deglaze the pan and bubble for a few seconds. Drizzle the sticky syrup over the vegetables and serve.

(Y) **Vegetarian tip:** replace the cooked chicken with 60 g (2 oz) Quorn deli style wafer thin chicken in step 3, for a **POINTS** value of $^1/_2$ per serving.

Three green bean salad

Takes 30 minutes *Serves 2*

4 POINTS *values per recipe*

185 calories *per serving*

75 g (2³/₄ oz) bulgar wheat

50 g (1³/₄ oz) fine green beans *trimmed and halved*

50 g (1³/₄ oz) runner beans *trimmed and sliced*

100 g (3¹/₂ oz) sugar snap peas

a generous pinch of dried chilli flakes

1 tablespoon finely chopped fresh chives

1 tablespoon finely chopped fresh flat leaf parsley

1 tablespoon lemon juice

¹/₂ teaspoon granulated artificial sweetener

200 g (7 oz) tinned cherry tomatoes in tomato juice

salt and freshly ground black pepper

① Bring a pan of water to the boil, add the bulgar wheat and then bring back to the boil. Simmer for 10–15 minutes until tender.

② Meanwhile, bring another pan of water to the boil. Add the green beans and runner beans and simmer for 2 minutes. Add the sugar snap peas and cook for 1 more minute. Drain and rinse with cold water. Drain again.

③ When the bulgar wheat is tender, drain and rinse in cold water until the bulgar wheat is cold. Drain again, ensuring all the water has gone (use the bottom of a bowl to push out the water).

④ Transfer the bulgar wheat to a large bowl and mix in the chilli flakes, fresh chopped herbs, lemon juice, sweetener and cherry tomatoes and juice. Fold through the cooked beans, season and serve.

Super speedy day

Breakfast **Speedy scrambled eggs:** whisk together 1 tsp tomato purée, 1 egg and 1 tbsp skimmed milk. Spray a small non stick frying pan with low fat cooking spray and cook for 1 or 2 minutes until just set. Serve with grilled flat field mushrooms and rashers of lean back bacon. ¹/₂ a grapefruit.

Ⓨ *Lunch* **Three green bean salad:** (see recipe) drizzled with 1 tsp extra virgin olive oil to serve. A pear with a pot of low fat fruit fromage frais.

Dinner **Minty lamb:** mix together 1 tbsp low fat garlic and herb soft cheese and 1 tsp mint sauce. Season generously. Griddle or grill a lamb chop brushed with 1 tsp olive oil and serve with the creamy mint sauce, baby carrots, cooked potatoes and tender stem broccoli.

Ⓨ *Dessert* A pot of low fat yogurt and 1 banana.

Calcium guidelines Add 150 ml (5 fl oz) skimmed milk to this menu plan to keep your daily calcium intake at the recommended levels (see p. 80 of your Eat Wisely book).

Poached salmon with cucumber relish

Takes 15 minutes to prepare, 1 hour to cook *Serves 4*

14 *POINTS* values per recipe

210 calories per serving

450 g (1 lb) skinless salmon fillet

4 or 5 sprigs of fresh thyme, plus extra to garnish

1 bay leaf

15 black peppercorns

1 celery stick

1 onion *quartered*

1 litre (1³/₄ pints) diet lemonade

275 g (9¹/₂ oz) cucumber *halved, deseeded and sliced into moons*

2 tablespoons chopped fresh dill

1 tablespoon white wine vinegar

salt and freshly ground black pepper

① Put the salmon, thyme, bay leaf, peppercorns, celery, onion and diet lemonade into a wide, lidded pan. Bring to the boil and simmer for 5 minutes. Remove from the heat, cover and leave for 1 hour.

② Meanwhile, in a bowl mix together the cucumber, dill, 1 tablespoon hot water and vinegar. Season and set aside.

③ Remove the salmon from the cooking liquid with a fish slice and arrange on a platter. Scatter over the cucumber relish, season with freshly ground black pepper and garnish with thyme to serve.

Ⓥ **Vegetarian tip:** the cucumber relish is delicious with vegetarian cheese. Try serving it with wholemeal crispbreads and low fat soft cheese.

Lunch with friends

Ⓥ *Breakfast* A medium bowl of non sugary cereal served with skimmed milk. Grill 2 large flat mushrooms brushed with 2 tsp olive oil and serve with wilted spinach, mixed with 1 tbsp Quark.

Lunch **Poached salmon with cucumber relish:** (see recipe) served with boiled new potatoes, mixed with Italian fat free dressing. A large mixed salad.

Dinner **Ham with egg:** serve sliced tomatoes and thickly sliced ham, topped with poached egg.

Dessert **Peach melba fool:** whiz 75 g (2³/₄ oz) canned apricots in natural juice, a 120 g pot of Weight Watchers Peach Thick and Fruity Yogurt and 1 tbsp low fat soft cheese until smooth. Spoon into a dessert glass and chill until required.

Calcium guidelines Add 150 ml (5 fl oz) skimmed milk to this menu plan to keep your daily calcium intake at the recommended levels (see p. 80 of Eat Wisely).

Caribbean holiday

 Breakfast A medium bowl of non sugary cereal with skimmed milk and seasonal fruits, served with 0% fat Greek yogurt.

 Lunch **Caribbean rice:** (see recipe). A bowl of fresh cherries.

Dinner **Herbed chicken:** slice a skinless boneless chicken breast in half, while keeping it joined at one side, so that it opens up like a book. Put into a non metallic dish. Mix together the juice of $^1/_2$ a lemon, 1 crushed garlic clove, 2 tsp olive oil and 1 tsp mixed dried herbs. Pour over the chicken breast and leave for 15 minutes. Remove the chicken from the marinade and cook in a non stick frying pan or on a griddle pan for 10–15 minutes, turning once. Serve with courgettes, peppers and squash, sprayed with low fat cooking spray and roasted in the oven.

 Dessert **Frozen bananas:** cut a banana into chunks and thread on to cocktail skewers. Freeze for 30 minutes. Serve with a pot of low fat fruity yogurt, using the banana chunks for dipping.

Calcium guidelines Add 150 ml (5 fl oz) skimmed milk to this menu plan to keep your daily calcium intake at the recommended levels (see p. 80 of your Eat Wisely book).

Caribbean rice

Takes 45 minutes *Serves 2*

8 *POINTS* values per recipe
310 calories per serving

125 g (4$^1/_2$ oz) brown rice
75 g (2$^3/_4$ oz) frozen peas
$^1/_2$ red pepper *deseeded and sliced finely*
$^1/_2$ small red onion *diced finely*
125 g (4$^1/_2$ oz) fresh or canned pineapple in natural juice *cut into chunks*
2 tablespoons chopped fresh coriander
1 tomato *deseeded and diced finely*
2 tablespoons Italian style fat free dressing
salt and freshly ground black pepper

1 Put the brown rice into a large saucepan with lots of boiling water. Bring back to the boil and simmer for 30 minutes until tender. Drain and rinse in cold water until the rice is cold. Drain again thoroughly.

2 Meanwhile, put the frozen peas into a bowl and pour over boiling water. Leave for 5 minutes. Drain and put into a large bowl.

3 Add the rice to the peas along with the pepper, onion, pineapple, coriander and tomato. Stir though the Italian dressing, season to taste and serve.

Cheat's soup

Takes 20 minutes *Serves 4*

8¹/₂ *POINTS* values per recipe

165 calories *per serving*

low fat cooking spray

1 onion *chopped finely*

1 red pepper *deseeded and sliced*

1 tablespoon mild or hot curry powder

1 x 700 g jar of passata with onion and garlic

50 g (1³/₄ oz) fine green beans *trimmed and halved*

300 ml (10 fl oz) hot beef stock

1 x 410 g can of chickpeas *drained and rinsed*

3 x 30 g (1¹/₄ oz) medium slices of cooked roast beef *shredded*

2 tablespoons chopped fresh coriander, plus extra to garnish

salt and freshly ground black pepper

1 Heat a deep saucepan and spray with low fat cooking spray. Gently cook the onion and pepper for 5 minutes until softened. Add the curry powder, passata, green beans and beef stock and bring to the boil. Simmer for 5 minutes, stirring occasionally.

2 Add the chickpeas and shredded beef, reserving a few shreddings for garnish. Cook for 1–2 minutes or until heated through. Check the seasoning, stir in the coriander and serve garnished with the reserved beef shreddings and the remaining coriander.

Ⓨ Vegetarian tip: in step 2, replace the roast beef with 100 g (3¹/₂ oz) diced tofu. Spray a non stick frying pan with low fat cooking spray and fry the tofu until golden, for a *POINTS* value of 1¹/₂ per serving.

* If you haven't already included your oil, this is a great recipe for including some of your 2 tsp of healthy oil a day; in step 1 simply replace the low fat cooking spray with 2 tsp sunflower oil.

Fresh food fast

Ⓨ *Breakfast* **Peach smoothie:** whiz 50 g (1³/₄ oz) raspberries, a 210 g can of peaches in natural juice and 75 ml (3 fl oz) skimmed milk until smooth.

Lunch **Cheat's soup:** (see recipe) served with wholewheat crispbreads, spread with low fat soft cheese. 1 pear. A pot of low fat plain yogurt.

Dinner **Cheesy topped pork:** brush a pork loin steak with 1 tsp olive oil and grill for 10 minutes, turning after 5 minutes. Meanwhile, mix together low fat soft cheese, a pinch of cayenne pepper and snipped fresh chives. Season. Top the pork steak with a small sliced tomato. Brush with 1 tsp olive oil. Grill for 3 minutes. Spread over the cheese mixture. Grill for 1 minute. Serve with a jacket potato and courgettes.

Ⓨ *Dessert* A handful of mixed grapes with very low fat fruit fromage frais.

Calcium guidelines Add 150 ml (5 fl oz) skimmed milk to this menu plan to keep your daily calcium intake at the recommended levels (see p. 80 of your Eat Wisely book).

Crab coleslaw

Takes 20 minutes *Serves 4*

12^1/$_2$ POINTS *values per recipe*

180 calories *per serving*

2 x 170 g cans of white crab meat in brine

^{1}/$_2$ red onion *sliced finely*

1 apple *cored and sliced finely*

150 g (5^1/$_2$ oz) white cabbage *cored and shredded finely*

75 g (2^3/$_4$ oz) cucumber *sliced finely*

1 x 25 g packet of fresh coriander *chopped roughly*

1 small carrot *peeled and grated*

1 avocado *peeled, stoned and sliced thinly*

salt and freshly ground black pepper

For the dressing

zest and juice of 2 limes

4 tablespoons low fat plain fromage frais

1 teaspoon tomato purée

a few drops of Tabasco

^{1}/$_2$ teaspoon Worcestershire sauce

1 In a bowl, mix together all the dressing ingredients and season. Set aside.

2 Drain one can of crab meat and empty into a large bowl. Mix in the onion, apple, cabbage, cucumber, coriander and carrot.

3 Add the dressing and toss gently to combine. Divide the avocado between four plates and top each with a generous amount of the crab coleslaw. Drain the remaining can of crab meat and crumble over the top of each salad.

Salad days

Ⓨ *Breakfast* Coffee made with skimmed milk from your daily allowance. Wholewheat crispbreads spread with low fat soft cheese mashed with a banana.

Lunch **Crab coleslaw:** (see recipe). An orange and a pot of low fat fruit yogurt.

Ⓨ *Dinner* **Quorn spaghetti bolognese:** heat 2 tsp olive oil in a saucepan. Cook ^{1}/$_2$ an onion, 1 diced carrot, ^{1}/$_2$ a diced courgette and ^{1}/$_4$ diced red pepper for 5–8 minutes until starting to soften. Add 100 g (3^1/$_2$ oz) Quorn mince, a 200 g can of chopped tomatoes, 1 tsp Herb and Garlic Italian seasoning, 1 tbsp soy sauce, 1 tsp tomato purée and 100 ml (3^1/$_2$ fl oz) vegetable stock. Simmer for 20 minutes. Serve with cooked spaghetti and a green salad.

Ⓨ *Dessert* **Roasted figs:** put 2 halved figs on a baking tray and top with 1 tsp lemon juice, 1 tsp thyme leaves and ^{1}/$_2$ tsp granulated artificial sweetener. Roast in a preheated oven at 200°C for 10 minutes. Serve with a pot of low fat plain yogurt.

Springtime veggies

Ⓨ *Breakfast* A medium bowl of non sugary cereal served with skimmed milk and a sliced banana.

Ⓨ *Lunch* **Mixed plate:** mix together low fat plain cottage cheese with snipped fresh chives, a deseeded, diced tomato and a deseeded, diced pepper. Serve with wholewheat crispbreads. A satsuma and a handful of grapes.

Ⓨ *Dinner* **Primavera pasta:** (see recipe) served with a mixed salad, drizzled with 2 tsp olive oil mixed with $^1/_2$ tsp mustard and 1 tsp white wine vinegar.

Ⓨ *Dessert* **Indian spiced pineapple kebab:** thread cubed, fresh pineapple on to a skewer. Mix together 1 tsp granulated artificial sweetener with the crushed seeds from 2 cardamom pods. Sprinkle this over the pineapple and grill for 5 minutes until starting to caramelize. Serve with a pot of low fat plain fromage frais.

Calcium guidelines Add 150 ml (5 fl oz) skimmed milk to this menu plan to keep your daily calcium intake at the recommended levels (see p. 80 of your Eat Wisely book).

Primavera pasta

Takes 30 minutes *Serves 2*

Ⓨ

10$^1/_2$ POINTS *values per recipe*

400 calories *per serving*

100 g (3$^1/_2$ oz) dried spaghetti
600 ml (1 pint) hot vegetable stock
1 small onion *chopped finely*
4 sprigs of fresh thyme
1 large garlic clove *sliced*
75 g (2$^3/_4$ oz) baby carrots *scrubbed and trimmed*
50 g (1$^3/_4$ oz) frozen petit pois
50 g (1$^3/_4$ oz) frozen broad beans
1 small courgette *trimmed and sliced finely*
50 g (1$^3/_4$ oz) fine asparagus *trimmed and cut into 2.5 cm (1 inch) pieces*
4 tablespoons low fat soft cheese
1 egg yolk
salt and freshly ground black pepper

① Bring a saucepan of water to the boil and cook the spaghetti for 10–12 minutes or according to packet instructions until 'al dente'. Drain and return the spaghetti to the pan.

② Meanwhile, in a separate saucepan, bring the vegetable stock to the boil and add the onion, thyme, garlic and carrots. Bring back to the boil and simmer for 5 minutes.

③ Add the petit pois, broad beans and courgette to the stock. Bring back to the boil and simmer for 2 minutes. Add the asparagus and simmer for a further minute. Drain and add to the cooked spaghetti in the pan, reserving 100 ml (3$^1/_2$ fl oz) cooking liquid.

④ Mix the reserved cooking liquid with the soft cheese and egg yolk. Return to the pan with the spaghetti and cook for 1 minute until slightly thickened. Season and serve immediately.

Cajun style chicken drummers

Takes 15 minutes to prepare + 1 hour marinating, 45 minutes to cook

Serves 4

12 POINTS values per recipe

215 calories *per serving*

2 teaspoons coriander seeds *crushed*

1 teaspoon ground cumin

1 teaspoon mild chilli powder

1 teaspoon herbes de Provence

¹/₂ teaspoon paprika

1 teaspoon ground allspice

2 teaspoons Dijon mustard

2 tablespoons low fat plain yogurt

8 chicken drumsticks *skin removed*

For the sweetcorn salsa

1 x 198 g can of sweetcorn *drained*

2 vine tomatoes *deseeded and chopped roughly*

1 teaspoon granulated artificial sweetener

1 tablespoon white wine vinegar

1 red onion *chopped finely*

❶ In a bowl, mix together all the spices, mustard and yogurt. Score three shallow cuts into each chicken drumstick and put into a large freezer bag. Add the yogurt and spices and massage into the chicken drumsticks. Leave to marinate for at least 1 hour.

❷ Preheat the oven to Gas Mark 5/190°C/fan oven 170°C and line a baking tray with foil. Put the chicken drumsticks on the baking tray and bake in the oven for 40–45 minutes, until cooked and the juices run clear.

❸ Meanwhile, mix together all the salsa ingredients and chill until needed. Serve with the chicken drumsticks.

Finger food

Ⓨ *Breakfast* A medium bowl of porridge made with skimmed milk and served with fresh raspberries.

Ⓨ *Lunch* **Jacket potato:** fill a jacket potato with reduced sugar and salt baked beans. Serve with a large mixed salad. A banana. A pot of low fat yogurt.

Dinner **Cajun style chicken drummers:** (see recipe) served with mixed stir fried vegetables, cooked with 2 tsp sunflower oil.

Ⓨ *Dessert* **Tangy strawberries:** heat hulled, halved strawberries in a pan with 1 tbsp balsamic vinegar for 1 or 2 minutes until syrupy and top with 1 tbsp low fat fromage frais.

Calcium guidelines Add 150 ml (5 fl oz) skimmed milk to this menu plan to keep your daily calcium intake at the recommended levels (see p. 80 of your Eat Wisely book).

Stir fried beef noodles

Takes 30 minutes *Serves 2*

12¹/₂ POINTS *values per recipe*

445 calories *per serving*

100 g (3¹/₂ oz) medium rice noodles

low fat cooking spray

¹/₂ small red onion *sliced*

1 red chilli *deseeded and diced*

2 garlic cloves *sliced*

2 x 110 g (4 oz) lean fillet steak *sliced finely*

¹/₂ red pepper *deseeded and sliced finely*

125 g (4¹/₂ oz) mange tout

juice of 2 limes

2 tablespoons Thai fish sauce

1 teaspoon lemongrass purée (oil free)

1 egg *beaten*

2 spring onions *sliced finely*

2 tablespoons chopped fresh coriander

1 Cook the noodles in boiling water according to packet instructions. Drain and rinse in cold water. Set aside.

2 Heat a wok until hot. Spray with low fat cooking spray. Stir fry the onion, chilli and garlic for 2–3 minutes. Add the steak. Stir fry for 1 minute, stirring constantly. Add the pepper and mange tout. Cook for 2 minutes. Pour in the lime juice, fish sauce and lemongrass purée, bubble for a few seconds and then toss through the cooked noodles.

3 Pour in the beaten egg and allow the mixture to set for 1 minute. Quickly stir to shred the egg and serve scattered with the spring onions and coriander.

* If you haven't already included your oil, this is a great recipe for including some of your 2 tsp of healthy oil a day; in step 2 simply replace the low fat cooking spray with 2 tsp sunflower oil.

Oriental delights

Ⓨ *Breakfast* A medium bowl of non sugary cereal with skimmed milk. 2 clementines.

Lunch **Ham and cheese bruschetta:** wholewheat crispbreads topped with low fat garlic and chive soft cheese and scrunched Parma ham or wafer thin ham. A low fat fruit fromage frais. An apple. A slice of melon.

Dinner **Stir fried beef noodles:** (see recipe).

Ⓨ *Dessert* **Exotic fruit salad:** whiz 1 peeled and chopped kiwi with 1 tbsp low fat plain yogurt until puréed. Pour this over peeled and stoned lychees, a peeled, stoned and sliced mango and some canned tropical fruit salad in natural juice.

Calcium guidelines Add 150 ml (5 fl oz) skimmed milk to this menu plan to keep your daily calcium intake at the recommended levels (see p. 80 of your Eat Wisely book).

Mediterranean memories

Ⓨ *Breakfast* Serve warmed plum tomatoes and low fat cottage cheese with wholewheat crispbreads. A latte made with hot skimmed milk from your daily allowance, whipped with a milk frother and mixed with 1 tsp instant coffee. Fresh raspberries.

Lunch **Ham salad with pasta:** top $^1/_2$ a peeled, stoned and sliced avocado with a diced tomato, wafer thin ham, a few basil leaves and a generous handful of mixed salad leaves. Drizzle with 1 tbsp mature balsamic vinegar mixed with 2 tsp extra virgin olive oil. Serve with cooked wholewheat pasta. An orange. A pot of low fat fruit yogurt.

Dinner **Tangy lamb souvlaki:** (see recipe) served with brown rice and a generous mixed salad.

Ⓨ *Dessert* **Fruit salad:** a sliced apple and pear with seedless grapes.

Calcium guidelines Add 150 ml (5 fl oz) skimmed milk to this menu plan to keep your daily calcium intake at the recommended levels (see p. 80 of your Eat Wisely book).

Tangy lamb souvlaki

Takes 50 minutes + 30 minutes marinating *Serves 4*

12$^1/_2$ POINTS *values per recipe*
160 calories *per serving*

8 long, tough fresh rosemary sprigs (for skewers)
250 g (9 oz) fresh apricots *stoned and chopped roughly*
2 tablespoons white wine vinegar
2 garlic cloves
1 tablespoon granulated artificial sweetener
$^1/_2$ teaspoon ground allspice
4 x 125 g (4$^1/_2$ oz) lean lamb leg steaks *cut into bite size chunks*
600 g (1 lb 5 oz) cooked brown rice *to serve*

① To make skewers, starting about 2.5 cm (1 inch) down from the top of each rosemary sprig, remove the leaves and reserve the stalks and 1 tablespoon of the removed leaves. Discard the remaining leaves. (You can also use wooden skewers instead of rosemary skewers).

② Put the reserved rosemary leaves into a small lidded pan along with the apricots, vinegar, 100 ml (3$^1/_2$ fl oz) water, garlic, sweetener and allspice. Bring to the boil, cover and simmer for 5–10 minutes until stewed. Leave to cool for 20 minutes.

③ Meanwhile, thread the chunks of lamb on to the stripped rosemary skewers, leaving the rosemary leaves exposed at the top (or thread on to wooden skewers). Put into a shallow non metallic dish.

④ When the stewed apricots are cool, whiz in a food processor or with a hand blender until puréed. Pour half over the lamb skewers and leave for 30 minutes.

⑤ Preheat the grill to medium high and grill (or barbecue) the lamb skewers for 10–15 minutes, basting with the marinade until cooked and starting to caramelize. Transfer the skewers to the plate with the reserved glaze as a chutney on the side. Serve 150 g (5$^1/_2$ oz) cooked brown rice per person for an additional **POINTS** value of 3 per serving.

Baked chicken lentils

Takes 20 minutes to prepare, 45 minutes to cook

Serves 4

36¹/₂ POINTS values per recipe

440 calories per serving

low fat cooking spray

4 x 250 g (9 oz) skinless chicken leg quarters

1 onion *sliced finely*

1 garlic clove *crushed*

2 rashers of lean back bacon *chopped*

1 x 210 g can of green lentils in brine *drained and rinsed*

200 ml (7 fl oz) chicken stock

1 tablespoon tomato purée

4 tablespoons balsamic vinegar

¹/₂ tablespoon dried tarragon

1 tablespoon vegetable gravy granules

4 large vine tomatoes *quartered*

freshly ground black pepper

① Preheat the oven to Gas Mark 4/180°C/fan oven 160°C. Heat a flame and ovenproof lidded casserole dish and spray with low fat cooking spray. Cook the chicken for 5 minutes, until brown all over. Remove.

② Spray the casserole dish again with low fat cooking spray and cook the onion, garlic and bacon for 4 minutes until starting to soften.

③ Add the lentils, chicken stock, tomato purée, vinegar, tarragon and gravy granules. Cover and bring to the boil. Return the chicken pieces to the top and bake in the oven for 20 minutes.

④ Remove from the oven and scatter over the tomato quarters. Return to the oven for a further 25 minutes until cooked and the sauce is thickened. Adjust the seasoning and serve.

Variation: use 4 x 165 g (5³/₄ oz) skinless boneless chicken breasts instead of leg quarters for a **POINTS** value of 4 per serving.

Saturday night in

Ⓨ *Breakfast* **Morning rosti:** preheat the oven to 220ºC. Heat 1 tsp oil in a non stick frying pan. Grate 100 g (3¹/₂ oz) cold, boiled potatoes and a peeled, cored apple into a bowl. Season. Put 3 large spoonfuls into the pan, flatten and cook gently for 10–15 minutes, turning once. Serve with a soft boiled egg and cherry tomatoes, brushed with 1 tsp olive oil, and roasted in the preheated oven. A 150 ml (5 fl oz) glass of skimmed milk.

Ⓨ *Lunch* **Vegetable soup:** a bowl of non creamy vegetable soup. Wholewheat crispbreads with low fat soft cheese. A kiwi. A handful of grapes.

Dinner **Baked chicken lentils:** (see recipe) served with spinach, runner beans and carrots.

Ⓨ *Dessert* **Sweet berries:** warm frozen mixed berries with 1 tsp vanilla extract for 2–3 minutes. Stir in ¹/₂ tsp artificial sweetener. A pot of 0% fat Greek yogurt.

Calcium guidelines Add 150 ml (5 fl oz) skimmed milk to this menu plan to keep your daily calcium intake at the recommended levels (see p. 80 of your Eat Wisely book).

Stuffed pork loin

Takes 40 minutes to prepare, 1¹/₂ hours to cook

Serves 4

17¹/₂ POINTS *values per recipe*

350 calories *per serving*

600 g (1 lb 5 oz) lean pork loin joint *fat trimmed to a thin layer*

juice and zest of ¹/₂ a lemon

30 g (1¹/₄ oz) bulgar wheat

low fat cooking spray

2 shallots *chopped finely*

1 small eating apple *cored and diced*

8 fresh sage leaves *chopped*

7 black olives in brine *drained and chopped finely*

3 tablespoons low fat soft cheese

salt and freshly ground black pepper

1 Preheat the oven to Gas Mark 5/190°C/fan oven 170°C. Put the pork on a board, with the fat at the top. Cut the pork about 1 cm (¹/₂ inch) below the top of the pork lengthways, then turn the knife and cut around in a spiral, eventually enabling you to roll the meat out flat. Put the pork in a shallow dish, cut side up and sprinkle with the lemon zest and juice. Set aside.

2 To make the stuffing, put the bulgar wheat into a pan of boiling water and simmer for 15 minutes until tender. Drain.

3 Meanwhile, heat a non stick frying pan and spray with low fat cooking spray. Cook the shallots, apple and sage for 5–8 minutes until softened. Put into a bowl.

4 Stir in the bulgar wheat, olives and soft cheese and season. Cool. Spoon the stuffing along the length of the pork. Re-roll the pork and tie with kitchen string in about 5 places. If any stuffing comes out, squidge it back in.

5 Place in a roasting tin, cover with foil and roast for 45 minutes. Remove the foil and roast for a further 30–40 minutes or until cooked. Carve in thick slices and serve.

Sunday roast

Ⓨ *Breakfast* **Banana smoothie:** soak 1 Weetabix in skimmed milk. Whiz the soaked Weetabix with 1 peeled, chopped small banana and a pot of low fat fruit yogurt (such as raspberry) until smooth.

Lunch **Bacon and eggs:** serve poached eggs with grilled lean back bacon rashers, grilled tomato halves and a can of reduced sugar and salt baked beans in tomato sauce.

Dinner **Stuffed pork loin:** (see recipe) served with carrots, cauliflower, peas and potatoes roasted in 2 tsp sunflower oil.

Ⓨ *Dessert* Low fat fruit fromage frais and slices of cantaloupe melon.

Fish in a flash

Y *Breakfast* **Berry smoothie:** whiz 75 g (2³/₄ oz) frozen or fresh raspberries with 4 tbsp skimmed milk and 75 g (2³/₄ oz) low fat plain yogurt in a food processor or with a hand blender. 1 nectarine and wholewheat crispbreads with very low fat soft cheese.

Lunch **Loaded skins:** preheat the oven to 220°C. Prick a potato all over with a fork. Microwave on high for 8 minutes until tender. Leave to cool for 5 minutes. Cut the potato into quarters and scoop out nearly all the potato flesh and put into a bowl. Drizzle the potato skins with 2 tsp sunflower oil and bake in preheated oven for 10–15 minutes until crispy. Meanwhile, mash the cooked potato flesh and mix with chopped wafer thin chicken, low fat onion and chive cottage cheese and seasoning. Serve with the potato skins and a generous mixed salad. A pear.

Dinner **Chunky fish fingers:** (see recipe) served with tomato halves, grilled under a hot grill for a few minutes, carrots and sweetcorn.

Dessert **Lemon jelly:** serve lemon and lime sugar free jelly with a pot of low fat fruit fromage frais.

Calcium guidelines Add 150 ml (5 fl oz) skimmed milk to this menu plan to keep your daily calcium intake at the recommended levels (see p. 80 of your Eat Wisely book).

Chunky fish fingers

Takes 35 minutes *Serves 4*

❄ *recommended for fish fingers only*
19 POINTS *values per recipe*
260 calories *per serving*

8 x 15 g (¹/₂ oz) wholewheat crispbreads
4 x 100 g (3¹/₂ oz) skinless cod loin fillets *each cut into 2 or 3 long fingers*
1 egg *beaten*
250 g (9 oz) frozen peas
¹/₂ x 25 g packet of fresh mint *leaves only*
For the tartare sauce
juice of ¹/₂ a lemon
4 tablespoons Quark
1 tablespoon low fat plain yogurt
1 tablespoon chopped fresh dill
1 teaspoon capers *drained and chopped finely*
25 g (1 oz) cocktail gherkins *chopped finely*

1 Put the wholewheat crispbreads into a food processor and whiz until fine crumbs or use a hand blender. Transfer to a shallow dish. Dip the cod pieces in the wholewheat crumbs, coating them thoroughly. Dip the cod pieces into the beaten egg and then back into the crumbs, ensuring they are completely coated.

2 Preheat the grill to medium high and grill the fish fingers for 10 minutes, turning once halfway through.

3 Meanwhile, put the peas into a pan of boiling water and bring to the boil. Simmer for 3 minutes or until tender. Drain the peas and then whiz them in the food processor briefly with the mint leaves, until half puréed. Keep warm.

4 Mix together all the ingredients for the tartare sauce in a bowl and serve with the fish fingers and mushy peas.

Turkey terrine

Takes 20 minutes to prepare, 1 hour to cook *Serves 6*

25 POINTS values per recipe

235 calories per serving

10 slices of Parma ham

450 g (1 lb) lean turkey mince

4 egg yolks

250 g (9 oz) Quark

1 tablespoon mixed peppercorns in brine *drained*

1 tablespoon dried tarragon

① Preheat the oven to Gas Mark 3/160°C/fan oven 140°C. Line a 900 g (2 lb) loaf tin with the slices of Parma ham, ensuring that the joins overlap, that there are no gaps and leaving the ends overhanging the edge of the tin.

② In a large bowl, mix together the turkey mince, egg yolks, Quark, peppercorns and tarragon until combined. Spoon into the loaf tin, pressing down with the back of a spoon. Fold the overhanging lengths of Parma ham back over the meat to wrap up. Fill the kettle with water and turn on to boil.

③ Put the loaf tin into a roasting tray and fill the tray two thirds the way up the sides of the loaf tin with boiling water. Bake in the oven for 1 hour or until the juices run clear.

④ Drain the liquid away from the tray and turn the loaf out on to a plate. Wipe away the milky residue with damp kitchen paper. Carve into slices and serve warm or leave to go cold and then slice.

Ploughman's fare

Ⓨ *Breakfast* **Iced juice:** whiz a peeled and cored apple and a can of mandarin segments in natural juice in a blender until smooth. Serve in a glass with ice. Wholewheat crispbreads with low fat soft cheese.

Lunch **Creamy prawn salad:** scatter sliced radishes, sliced pepper, diced cucumber and canned sweetcorn over some lettuce. Top with cooked prawns mixed with low fat plain cottage cheese to serve. Whiz together 75 g (2³/₄ oz) raspberries with 150 ml (5 fl oz) skimmed milk and a banana to make a smoothie.

Dinner **Turkey terrine:** (see recipe) served with cooked new potatoes, tossed with 2 tsp olive oil, 1 tbsp chopped parsley, pickled gherkins and pickled onions.

Ⓨ *Dessert* **Semolina with apricots:** microwave on high 25 g (1 oz) semolina with 150 ml (5 fl oz) skimmed milk for 2 minutes until thickened, stirring every 30 seconds. Leave to stand for 1 minute and serve with a can of apricot halves in natural juice. A pot of low fat fruit fromage frais.

Chinese chicken

Takes 30 minutes *Serves 4*

9½ POINTS values per recipe

205 calories per serving

4 x 150 g (5½ oz) skinless boneless chicken breasts *cut into small chunks*

1 garlic clove *crushed*

2.5 cm (1 inch) piece of fresh ginger *peeled and grated*

2 tablespoons soy sauce

juice of ½ a lemon

low fat cooking spray

1 green pepper *deseeded and sliced*

1 carrot *peeled and sliced finely*

½ red chilli *deseeded and sliced finely*

1 onion *sliced*

100 ml (3½ fl oz) white wine vinegar

2 tablespoons granulated artificial sweetener

100 ml (3½ fl oz) passata

2 spring onions *sliced finely*

1 Put the chicken chunks in a non metallic bowl and mix with garlic, ginger, 1 tablespoon soy sauce and lemon juice.

2 Heat a wok until hot. Spray with low fat cooking spray and stir fry the chicken for 5 minutes until starting to brown. Add the pepper, carrot, chilli and onion and stir fry for a further 3 minutes.

3 Add the vinegar, sweetener, passata and remaining soy sauce. Cook for 2 minutes until starting to thicken. Sprinkle over the spring onions.

Serving suggestion: serve with a portion of egg fried rice (see opposite) for a **POINTS** value of 2½ per serving.

* If you haven't already included your oil, this is a great recipe for including some of your 2 tsp of healthy oil a day; in step 2 simply replace the low fat cooking spray with 2 tsp sunflower oil.

Summer sensations

Y *Breakfast* **Summer fruit swirl:** defrost 75 g (2¾ oz) frozen summer fruits. Whiz 25 g (1 oz) in a blender with 3 tbsp skimmed milk. In a glass, layer a pot of low fat fruit yogurt, the fruit purée and remaining fruits. Swirl a skewer through the glass to marble the yogurt.

Lunch **Cooling tuna pâté:** whiz a can of drained tuna in brine with low fat plain cottage cheese, chopped spring onion, chopped cucumber and lemon juice until smooth. Season and serve with wholewheat crispbreads, a baby leaf salad, cherry tomatoes and celery sticks. An orange.

Dinner **Chinese chicken:** (see recipe) served with egg fried rice. To make the fried rice, heat a wok until very hot and then spray with low fat cooking spray. Add 145 g (5¼ oz) cooked cold brown rice, 3 finely chopped spring onions and cook for 2 minutes, stirring. Add 1 lightly beaten egg and 75 g (2¾ oz) petit pois. Cook for 2 minutes, stirring to break up the egg. Transfer to a serving dish and keep warm. (Serves 4).

Y *Dessert* 3 ripe plums and a pot of low fat fromage frais.

Beside the seaside

Y *Breakfast* **Cinnamon grapefruit:** mix together $^1/_2$ tsp granulated artificial sweetener with a pinch of ground cinnamon. Sprinkle this over $^1/_2$ a grapefruit and grill for 2–3 minutes until starting to caramelize.

Lunch **Roast beef salad:** toss together slices of cooked roast beef, drained and sliced olives in brine, 2 tsp olive oil mixed with $^1/_2$ tsp horseradish sauce and 1 tsp white wine vinegar. Serve on top of a generous handful of salad leaves. A chopped mango and low fat plain yogurt.

Dinner **Zesty seafood shells:** (see recipe) served with a large mixed leaf salad, sweetcorn, radish, peppers and tomatoes.

Y *Dessert* **Pineapple carpaccio:** thinly slice fresh pineapple on to a plate. Drizzle with $^1/_2$ tsp vanilla extract and the zest of $^1/_4$ orange. Serve with low fat fruit yogurt.

Calcium guidelines Add 150 ml (5 fl oz) skimmed milk to this menu plan to keep your daily calcium intake at the recommended levels (see p. 80 of your Eat Wisely book).

Zesty seafood shells

Takes 35 minutes *Serves 2*

11 *POINTS* values per recipe
390 calories per serving

125 g (4$^1/_2$ oz) large pasta shells
low fat cooking spray
1 garlic clove *crushed*
50 g (1$^3/_4$ oz) baby spinach *rinsed*
4 vine ripened tomatoes *deseeded and diced*
150 g (5$^1/_2$ oz) cooked seafood medley (containing prawns, squid and mussels)
75 g (2$^3/_4$ oz) cooked and peeled large king prawns
4 tablespoons low fat plain cottage cheese
zest of 1 lemon
salt and freshly ground black pepper

1 Bring a large saucepan of water to the boil and cook the pasta shells for 10–12 minutes or according to packet instructions until 'al dente'. Drain and return to the pan.
2 Meanwhile, heat a wide pan and spray with low fat cooking spray. Add the garlic, spinach, tomatoes, seafood and prawns and gently heat for 5 minutes.
3 Add the cottage cheese, lemon zest and cooked pasta shells. Mix together and heat through for a few minutes. Season and serve.

Lamb ragu

Takes 20 minutes to prepare, 1 hour to cook *Serves 4*

14 POINTS values per recipe

290 calories per serving

low fat cooking spray

400 g (14 oz) lean lamb leg steak *cubed*

1 onion *sliced*

175 g (6 oz) aubergine *diced*

2 x 400 g cans of plum tomatoes

1 x 410 g can of haricot beans in brine *drained and rinsed*

1 bouquet garni

1 tablespoon paprika

2 tablespoons finely chopped fresh flat leaf parsley

4 tablespoons 0% fat Greek yogurt

salt and freshly ground black pepper

① Preheat the oven to Gas Mark 4/180°C/fan oven 160°C. Heat a flame and ovenproof lidded pan and spray with low fat cooking spray. Cook the lamb (in batches) for 5 minutes, until browned all over. Remove with a slotted spoon and set aside. Keep warm.

② Add the sliced onion to the pan and cook gently for 3–4 minutes until softened. Add the aubergine and cook for a further 5 minutes. Return the lamb to the pan along with the tomatoes, haricot beans, bouquet garni and paprika. Bring to the boil, cover and then bake in the oven for 1 hour, stirring after 30 minutes.

③ Remove the bouquet garni, season, scatter over the parsley and serve with 1 tablespoon 0% fat Greek yogurt for each plate.

Midweek family meal

Ⓨ *Breakfast* Weetabix with hot skimmed milk, and a bowl of fresh strawberries.

Lunch **Ham and leek frittata:** heat a small non stick frying pan with 2 tsp sunflower oil. Gently fry $^1/_2$ a sliced leek and sliced mushrooms for 5 minutes until softened. Add diced ham, frozen peas, 2 eggs whisked with 2 tbsp skimmed milk and seasoning. Cook gently for 5–10 minutes until set. Serve with wild rocket salad. A pot of low fat fruit yogurt. An apple and a pear.

Dinner **Lamb ragu:** (see recipe) served with carrots, green beans and spinach.

Ⓨ *Dessert* **Mixed fruit salad:** prepare a salad of 1 sliced and stoned peach, a handful of grapes and a sliced banana. Serve topped with low fat fruit yogurt.

Calcium guidelines Add 150 ml (5 fl oz) skimmed milk to this menu plan to keep your daily calcium intake at the recommended levels (see p. 80 of your Eat Wisely book).

Root vegetable bake

Takes 40 minutes to prepare, 30 minutes to cook

Serves 2

9 POINTS *values per recipe*

315 calories *per serving*

250 g (9 oz) parsnips *peeled and sliced finely*

125 g (4¹/₂ oz) carrots *peeled and sliced finely*

1 leek *trimmed and sliced finely*

300 ml (10 fl oz) vegetable stock

2 egg yolks

1 tablespoon horseradish sauce

2 tablespoons finely chopped fresh flat leaf parsley

3 tablespoons Quark

100 g (3¹/₂ oz) Quorn pieces

low fat cooking spray

salt and freshly ground black pepper

1 Preheat the oven to Gas Mark 5/190°C/fan oven 170°C. Put the parsnips, carrots, leek and vegetable stock into a large saucepan. Cover with a tight fitting lid and bring to the boil. Simmer for 10 minutes until tender.

2 Drain the vegetables and reserve 50 ml (2 fl oz) cooking liquid. Mix the egg yolks, horseradish, parsley, Quark, reserved cooking liquid and seasoning together. Toss with the vegetables and Quorn pieces.

3 Spoon into an 850 ml (1¹/₂ pint) ovenproof dish, spray with low fat cooking spray and bake in the oven for 25–30 minutes until golden.

* *If you haven't already included your oil, this is a great recipe for including some of your 2 tsp of healthy oil a day; in step 3 simply replace the low fat cooking spray with 2 tsp sunflower oil brushed over the top.*

Vegetarian on a budget

Ⓨ *Breakfast* A bowl of non sugary cereal with skimmed milk and blueberries. A pot of low fat plain yogurt.

Ⓨ *Lunch* **Soya bean salad:** simmer 75 g (2³/₄ oz) quinoa in boiling water for 10 minutes. Add 75 g (2³/₄ oz) soya beans to the pan. Cook for 3–5 minutes. Drain, refresh in cold water. Mix the quinoa and beans with 2 tbsp low fat plain cottage cheese, 1 tbsp fresh mint and halved cherry tomatoes and season. A pot of low fat fruit fromage frais. An apple.

Ⓨ *Dinner* **Root vegetable bake:** (see recipe) served with peas and green beans.

Ⓨ *Dessert* **Fluffy rhubarb:** whisk 1 egg white with 1 tbsp artificial sweetener until soft peaks. Microwave 125 g (4¹/₂ oz) rhubarb for 2 minutes until stewed, sweeten to taste with artificial sweetener and add to egg whites. Chill for 30 minutes in a glass bowl.

Calcium guidelines Add 150 ml (5 fl oz) skimmed milk to this menu plan to keep your daily calcium intake at the recommended levels (see p. 80 of your Eat Wisely book).

Romantic dinner

(Y) *Breakfast* **Dippy eggs:** a soft boiled egg with blanched asparagus to dip. A glass of tomato juice. A bowl of non sugary cereal with skimmed milk.

Lunch **Tuna salad:** make a salad with mixed leaves, chopped tomatoes, sliced spring onions and a can of drained tuna. Wholewheat crispbreads spread with low fat pineapple cottage cheese. A handful of mixed seedless grapes.

Dinner Starter **Melon with ham:** (serves 2) arrange 1/2 a peeled and cubed cantaloupe melon and quartered figs on 2 plates. Top each plate with slices of crumpled Parma ham. Season generously and serve.

Main **Creamy steak dauphinois:** (see recipe) served with green beans and peas, tossed with 2 tsp extra virgin olive oil.

(Y) *Dessert* **Caramelized oranges:** (serves 2) peel 2 oranges and remove as much pith as possible. Thickly slice and cook, on a hot griddle pan or in a non stick frying pan for 2 minutes, turning once, until caramelized. Serve in bowls, each with a pot of low fat vanilla yogurt.

Calcium guidelines Add 150 ml (5 fl oz) skimmed milk to this menu plan to keep your daily calcium intake at the recommended levels (see p. 80 of your Eat Wisely book).

Creamy steak dauphinois

Takes 30 minutes + cooling to prepare, 20 minutes to cook *Serves 2*

12 *POINTS* *values per recipe*
345 calories *per serving*

2 x 150 g (5¹/₂ oz) lean fillet steak *slightly flattened*
low fat cooking spray
175 g (6 oz) potato *peeled and sliced thinly*
1 small red onion *sliced in rings*
100 ml (3¹/₂ fl oz) skimmed milk
1 garlic clove *sliced*
3 fresh thyme sprigs
2 tablespoons low fat soft cheese
salt and freshly ground black pepper

① Preheat the oven to Gas Mark 5/190°C/fan oven 170°C and then preheat a baking tray in the oven. Heat a non stick frying pan (or griddle pan) until hot and spray the steaks with low fat cooking spray. Cook in the pan for 1 minute on each side, then transfer to a plate. Set aside.

② Put the potatoes, onions, milk, garlic and thyme into a saucepan. Cover and cook gently for 10–15 minutes on a low heat until nearly tender. Strain, reserving all the cooking liquid and transfer to a bowl. Discard the thyme sprigs.

③ Mix the low fat soft cheese with the reserved cooking liquid and season generously. Pour over the onions and potatoes and toss to coat. Leave to cool.

④ Carefully stack the onions and potatoes on top of each steak, remove the heated baking tray from the oven and then transfer the steaks to the baking tray. Bake in the oven for 15–20 minutes until the potatoes are golden. Sprinkle over some freshly ground black pepper and serve immediately.

(Y) **Vegetarian tip:** use the creamy potato and onion mixture to top two Quorn burgers as in step 4 for a **POINTS** value of 3 per serving.

Crunchy beef gratin

Takes 45 minutes to prepare, 45 minutes to cook

Serves 4

❄ *beef mixture only*

18 POINTS *values per recipe*

295 calories *per serving*

low fat cooking spray

500 g (1 lb 2 oz) lean diced stewing beef

1 onion *chopped finely*

1 garlic clove *crushed*

1 tablespoon tomato purée

1 tablespoon Worcestershire sauce

1 tablespoon whole grain mustard

150 g (5¹/₂ oz) baby carrots

600 ml (1 pint) beef stock

1 tablespoon beef gravy granules

450 g (1 lb) potatoes *peeled and cut into 1 cm (¹/₂ inch) cubes*

salt and freshly ground black pepper

1. Heat a large saucepan and spray with low fat cooking spray. Cook the beef in batches for 5 minutes until brown all over. Remove and set aside. Spray the pan again with low fat cooking spray and gently cook the onion and garlic for 3–4 minutes until softened.

2. Return the beef to the pan and add the tomato purée, Worcestershire sauce, mustard, carrots and stock. Bring to the boil and simmer for 20 minutes. Stir in the gravy granules and season.

3. Meanwhile, preheat the oven to Gas Mark 5/190°C/fan oven 170°C. Put the potatoes in a pan and cover with cold water. Bring to the boil and simmer for 5–8 minutes. Drain and set aside.

4. Spoon the beef mixture into a 1.7 litre (3 pint) ovenproof dish and top with the cooked diced potatoes. Spray with low fat cooking spray and bake for 45 minutes until golden and crispy.

Autumnal feast

Ⓨ *Breakfast* A medium bowl of porridge made with skimmed milk. A pear.

Ⓨ *Lunch* **Warm veggie salad:** boil cauliflower florets, sliced carrot, deseeded and diced red chilli and mange tout in a pan for 5 minutes. Drain then toss with 1 tbsp rinsed, mixed pulses. Cover and keep warm. In a bowl over a pan of simmering water, whisk 1 tsp Dijon mustard, 2 tsp olive oil, 1 egg yolk, 2 tbsp water and 1 tbsp white wine vinegar until thickened. Pour over the salad. A satsuma. A pot of low fat plain yogurt.

Dinner **Crunchy beef gratin:** (see recipe) served with mashed parsnip and swede.

Dessert **Fizzy jelly:** dissolve ¹/₂ x 23 g packet of lemon and lime sugar free jelly with 150 ml (5 fl oz) boiling water. Add 150 ml (5 fl oz) diet lemonade. Pour into a bowl with 50 g (1³/₄ oz) grapes and chill until set.

Calcium guidelines Add 150 ml (5 fl oz) skimmed milk to this menu plan to keep your daily calcium intake at the recommended levels (see p. 80 of your Eat Wisely book).

Pork chops with chilli apple sauce

Takes 30 minutes *Serves 4*

15¹/₂ *POINTS* values per recipe

260 calories per serving

1 Bramley apple *peeled, cored and chopped*

2 tablespoons cider vinegar

low fat cooking spray

4 x 150 g (5¹/₂ oz) lean pork loin steaks

1 onion *chopped finely*

1 red chilli *deseeded and chopped finely*

150 g (5¹/₂ oz) button mushrooms *wiped and halved*

300 ml (10 fl oz) vegetable stock

1 eating apple *cored and sliced thinly*

2 tablespoons low fat soft cheese

1 tablespoon vegetable gravy granules

salt and freshly ground black pepper

thyme sprigs *to garnish*

1 To make the apple sauce, put the Bramley apple into a small lidded pan with the vinegar. Cover and gently cook for 5 minutes until soft and stewed. Purée with a hand blender and set aside.

2 Heat a wide non stick frying pan and spray with low fat cooking spray. Brown the pork steaks on each side for 2 minutes. Remove and set aside.

3 Add the onion, chilli and mushrooms to the pan and gently cook for 3–4 minutes until softened. Add the vegetable stock, apple slices, apple purée and soft cheese. Bring to the boil and stir in the gravy granules until thickened.

4 Return the pork steaks to the pan and simmer for 10 minutes until cooked. Season and scatter over the thyme.

Weekday supper

Ⓨ *Breakfast* A medium bowl of All Bran with skimmed milk. A can of apricots in natural fruit juice.

Lunch **Chicken and avocado salad:** serve wholewheat crispbreads with sliced, cooked chicken and a peeled, stoned and sliced avocado, drizzled with 2 tsp olive oil and 1 tsp balsamic vinegar. A peach. A pot of low fat fromage frais.

Dinner **Pork chops with chilli apple sauce:** (see recipe) served with mashed potato, green beans and spinach.

Ⓨ *Dessert* **Summer fruits:** whiz 75 g (2³/₄ oz) frozen summer fruits with 1 tbsp low fat soft cheese and 1 tsp lemon juice in a food processor or with a hand blender until smooth. Sweeten to taste with artificial sweetener and serve immediately.

Calcium guidelines Add 150 ml (5 fl oz) skimmed milk to this menu plan to keep your daily calcium intake at the recommended levels (see p. 80 of your Eat Wisely book).

Al fresco

Ⓨ *Breakfast* A medium bowl of puffed wheat with skimmed milk. $^1/_2$ a grapefruit.

Lunch **Chargrilled steak salad:** a lean sirloin steak, griddled until cooked and then sliced thinly. Serve with a large mixed salad and 1 tbsp 0% fat Greek yogurt mixed with 1 tsp horseradish sauce and 1 tsp mustard. A portion of fresh strawberries. A pot of low fat yogurt.

Dinner **Chunky fish kebabs:** thread cubed, chunky, skinless cod loin, a deseeded and cubed red pepper and a cubed mango on to a kebab stick. Mix together the zest and juice of 1 lime, 2 tsp olive oil and 1 tsp ground cumin. Brush over the kebab and grill or barbecue for 10–15 minutes until cooked. Serve with couscous, cooked according to packet instructions, and mixed with fresh herbs.

Vegan **Ⓨ** *Dessert* **Frozen fruit salad:** (see recipe).

Calcium guidelines Add 150 ml (5 fl oz) skimmed milk to this menu plan to keep your daily calcium intake at the recommended levels (see p. 80 of your Eat Wisely book).

Frozen fruit salad

Takes 15 minutes + 4 hours freezing *Serves 4*

Ⓨ *vegan* ❄ *ice cubes only*

5 POINTS *values per recipe*

80 calories *per serving*

200 g (7 oz) fresh raspberries
3 teaspoons granulated artificial sweetener
zest of $^1/_2$ an orange
200 g (7 oz) kiwi *peeled and chopped*
juice of 1 lime
200 g (7 oz) cantaloupe melon *deseeded, peeled and cubed*
1 ripe mango *peeled, stoned and sliced*
150 g (5$^1/_2$ oz) fresh strawberries *hulled and quartered*

❶ Whiz the raspberries in a food processor or with a hand blender until puréed, and then pass through a sieve. Sweeten the purée with 2 teaspoons artificial sweetener and the orange zest. Pour into six ice cube tray holes.

❷ Whiz the kiwi until puréed and sweeten with 1 teaspoon artificial sweetener and the juice of 1 lime. Pour into another six ice cube tray holes.

❸ Whiz the melon until puréed and pour into yet another six ice cube tray holes. Freeze all the ice cube trays for 4 hours or overnight until frozen.

❹ Empty the ice cubes into a large bowl and toss with the mango and strawberries. Serve immediately.

Fruit bakes

Takes 15 minutes to prepare, 30 minutes to bake

Serves 2

7 *POINTS* values per recipe

265 calories per serving

2 tablespoons granulated artificial sweetener

$^1/_2$ vanilla pod *seeds scraped out*

2 pears *cored and sliced*

75 g (2$^3/_4$ oz) fresh blackberries

200 ml (7 fl oz) skimmed milk

50 g (1$^3/_4$ oz) polenta

low fat cooking spray

200 g pot of low fat plain yogurt *to serve*

① Preheat the oven to Gas Mark 5/190°C/fan oven 170°C. For the vanilla syrup, mix 2 tablespoons of water with 1 tablespoon sweetener and vanilla seeds. Set aside.

② Divide the pear and blackberries between two 250 ml (9 fl oz) ovenproof dishes and pour over the vanilla syrup.

③ Put the milk in a saucepan and bring to the boil. Quickly stir in the polenta and remaining artificial sweetener and stir until thickened. Pour on top of the fruits, spray with low fat cooking spray and bake in the oven for 30 minutes until golden. Serve with the yogurt.

Delicious home baking

Breakfast **Grilled kipper:** grill a kipper and top with a poached egg. A glass of tomato juice.

Lunch **Gammon with pineapple:** griddle or cook a gammon steak, brushed with 1 tsp olive oil. Serve with a slice of canned pineapple and cooked peas tossed with 1 shredded Little Gem lettuce. Fresh apricots and a pot of low fat fromage frais.

Dinner **Turkey noodle salad:** cook the rice noodles according to the packet instructions. Drain and rinse in cold water. Toss with herb salad leaves, diced tomato, sliced celery stick, diced red pepper and sliced spring onion. Meanwhile, stir fry a thinly sliced turkey steak with 1 tsp olive oil for 5 minutes until crispy. Serve on top of the noodle salad and drizzle with warm soy sauce.

Ⓨ *Dessert* **Fruit bakes:** (see recipe).

Calcium guidelines Add 150 ml (5 fl oz) skimmed milk to this menu plan to keep your daily calcium intake at the recommended levels (see p. 80 of your Eat Wisely book).

Triple decker lolly

Takes 10 minutes + 5$^{1}/_{2}$ hours freezing *Makes 6*

 ❄

4 POINTS *values per recipe*

40 calories *per serving*

150 g (5$^{1}/_{2}$ oz) fresh strawberries *hulled*

2 x 100 g pots of Weight Watchers Cherry Layered Fromage Frais

1 x 120 g pot of low fat apricot yogurt

75 g (2$^{3}/_{4}$ oz) fresh raspberries

1   Put the strawberries in a food processor or use a hand blender to whiz until puréed. Pass through a sieve to remove the pips. Set aside.

2   Mix together both pots of fromage frais and apricot yogurt. Lay out 6 x 100 ml (3$^{1}/_{2}$ fl oz) lolly moulds and sticks. Put a spoonful of fromage frais mixture into the bottom of each lolly mould, then add a few raspberries, a lolly stick and freeze for 1 hour.

3   Remove from the freezer and pour over a little strawberry purée and freeze for a further 30 minutes. Repeat the layers again, using up the yogurt, raspberries and purée. Freeze for a final 4 hours or until frozen.

Midsummer treat

Ⓨ *Breakfast* **Porridge:** a medium bowl of porridge made with skimmed milk. A handful of grapes.

Ⓨ *Lunch* **Mushroom soup:** heat 2 tsp olive oil in a pan and cook 125 g (4$^{1}/_{2}$ oz) mixed sliced mushrooms, a chopped garlic clove and 1 tsp thyme leaves for 5 minutes. Add 200 ml (7 fl oz) vegetable stock and bring to the boil. Cover and simmer for 5 minutes. Transfer to a blender with 1 tbsp low fat soft cheese and whiz until smooth. Season and, if necessary, reheat to serve. 4 wholewheat crispbreads and a pot of low fat fruit fromage frais.

Dinner **Autumn duck:** heat a lidded pan and spray with low fat cooking spray. Gently cook $^{1}/_{2}$ a sliced, red onion and 100 g (3$^{1}/_{2}$ oz) peeled, cubed butternut squash for 5 minutes. Add 150 ml (5 fl oz) vegetable stock, the zest of an orange and 1 tbsp soy sauce. Cover and simmer for 15–20 minutes until the squash is tender. Stir in 1 tsp vegetable gravy granules and heat until thickened. Serve with 150 g (5$^{1}/_{2}$ oz) cooked, skinless duck breast, orange slices, green beans and Brussels sprouts.

Ⓨ *Dessert* **Triple decker lolly:** (see recipe).

Traditional favourites

ⓨ *Breakfast* **Poached strawberries:** put 150 g (5^{1}/$_{2}$ oz) strawberries into a pan and pour over 100 ml (3^{1}/$_{2}$ fl oz) water and 1 tbsp sugar free blackcurrant cordial. Simmer and poach for 1 minute. A medium bowl of non sugary cereal with skimmed milk.

ⓨ *Lunch* **Beetroot soup:** put ^{1}/$_{2}$ a chopped onion, 200 g (7 oz) chopped cooked beetroot in natural juice and 200 ml (7 fl oz) vegetable stock in a pan. Bring to the boil. Simmer for 10 minutes. Whiz in a food processor or with a hand blender until smooth and season. Reheat and serve with 0% fat Greek yogurt and 1 tbsp snipped fresh chives. Wholewheat crispbreads with low fat garlic and herb soft cheese and a mixed salad. Remainder of pot of 0% fat Greek yogurt.

Dinner **Lamb hot pot:** put cubed potato and cubed swede into a pan of cold water. Bring to the boil. Simmer for 20 minutes until tender. Drain and mash. Meanwhile, heat a non stick frying pan with 2 tsp olive oil. Gently cook 1 peeled, sliced carrot and 1 sliced leek for 10 minutes. Remove and set aside. Add lean lamb leg steak and pan fry for 15 minutes, turning until cooked through. Return the leeks and carrots to the pan. Add 100 ml (3^{1}/$_{2}$ fl oz) vegetable stock, 1 tsp dried rosemary and 1 tsp gravy granules. Bring to a simmer until thickened. Serve with the swede mash.

ⓨ *Dessert* **Queen of puddings:** (see recipe).

Calcium guidelines Add 150 ml (5 fl oz) skimmed milk to this menu plan to keep your daily calcium intake at the recommended levels (see p. 80 of your Eat Wisely book).

Queen of **puddings**

Takes 1 hour + 30 minutes soaking *Serves 4*

ⓨ

9 *POINTS* *values per recipe*
160 calories *per serving*

250 ml (9 fl oz) skimmed milk
50 g (1^{3}/$_{4}$ oz) oat bran
zest of 1 lemon
4 tablespoons granulated artificial sweetener
150 g (5^{1}/$_{2}$ oz) fresh blueberries
250 g (9 oz) fresh raspberries
3 eggs *separated*

❶ Heat the milk in a pan and bring just to the boil. Remove from the heat and add the oat bran, lemon zest and 1 tablespoon artificial sweetener. Leave to soak for 30 minutes.

❷ Meanwhile, put the blueberries and raspberries into a small pan and gently cook, stirring for 5 minutes until half the fruits have burst, releasing their juices. Set aside.

❸ Preheat the oven to Gas Mark 4/180°C/fan oven 160°C. Beat the egg yolks into the soaked oat bran and pour into a 1 litre (1^{3}/$_{4}$ pints) ovenproof dish. Bake for 30 minutes until just set. Then spread the cooked fruits over the oat mixture.

❹ In a clean bowl, whisk together the egg whites until foamy. Gradually whisk in the remaining artificial sweetener until stiff peaks are formed. Spoon over the top of the pudding, creating peaks with the back of a spoon (don't worry about spreading the meringue up against the edges – it's quite pretty to see some of the fruits) and bake in the oven for 10 minutes until golden.

Strawberry cheesecake

Takes 30 minutes + 2 hours cooling *Serves 8*

18¹/₂ POINTS *values per recipe*

120 calories *per serving*

3 x 15 g (¹/₂ oz) wholewheat crispbreads

low fat cooking spray

400 g (14 oz) low fat soft cheese

3 eggs

3 tablespoons granulated artificial sweetener

150 ml (5 fl oz) 0% fat Greek yogurt

1 tablespoon vanilla extract

¹/₄ x 23 g packet of sugar free strawberry jelly

150 ml (5 fl oz) boiling water

175 g (6 oz) fresh strawberries *hulled and sliced*

① Preheat the oven to Gas Mark 3/160°C/fan oven 140°C. Put the crispbreads in a food processor and whiz until fine crumbs. Spray an 18 cm (7 inch) loose bottom round cake tin with low fat cooking spray. Put the crumbs into the tin and shake the crumbs around the tin to coat. Empty out any excess and discard.

② Put the soft cheese, eggs, sweetener, yogurt and vanilla extract into a bowl and whisk until smooth. Pour into the cake tin and bake in the oven for 30 minutes until just set. It should have a slight wobble in the middle.

③ Leave to cool in the tin for 30 minutes. Meanwhile, dissolve the jelly into the boiling water and set aside. When both are cool, arrange the strawberry slices over the top of the cheesecake and pour over the jelly. Chill for at least 1¹/₂ hours until set. Remove from the tin and slice to serve.

Sweet dreams

Ⓨ *Breakfast* **Porridge:** a medium bowl of porridge made with skimmed milk and served with a can of cocktail fruit in natural juice.

Ⓨ *Lunch* **Miso soup with veggies:** put 1 sachet of miso soup into a pan with 300 ml (10 fl oz) boiling water. Boil again, then add these sliced vegetables: ¹/₄ red pepper, 15 g (¹/₂ oz) Chinese cabbage, 25 g (1 oz) mange tout and 50 g (1³/₄ oz) cubed silken tofu. Simmer for 5 minutes and season to taste with soy sauce. A banana. A pot of low fat fruit fromage frais.

Vegan **Ⓨ** *Dinner* **Butternut squash risotto:** heat a lidded pan with 2 tsp olive oil and gently cook ¹/₂ diced onion, 1 crushed garlic clove and 225 g (8 oz) cubed squash for 5 minutes. Add 60 g (2 oz) brown rice and 200 ml (7 fl oz) vegetable stock. Cover and cook for 20 minutes until tender and the liquid has nearly all gone. Stir in baby spinach and halved cherry tomatoes. Season with freshly ground black pepper.

Dessert **Strawberry cheesecake:** (see recipe).

Blackberry meringues

Takes 20 minutes to prepare, 30 minutes to bake + cooling *Makes 8*

Y

POINTS values per recipe

0 calories *per serving*

8 egg whites
4 tablespoons granulated artificial sweetener
200 g (7 oz) fresh blackberries
4 tablespoons 0% fat Greek yogurt

1 Preheat the oven to Gas Mark 2/150°C/fan oven 130°C and line a baking tray with non stick baking parchment.

2 In a clean bowl, whisk the egg whites until foamy but not soft peaks. Gradually whisk in the sweetener until soft to stiff peaks are formed (but not dry).

3 Put eight large spoonfuls of the meringue mixture on to the tray and put two blackberries into the centre of each one.

4 Bake in the oven on the middle shelf for 30 minutes then remove and leave the meringues to go cold. Meanwhile, whiz the remaining blackberries in a food processor or with a hand blender and pass through a sieve. Swirl into the yogurt and serve with the meringues (two per person).

Marvellous meringues

Y *Breakfast* A medium bowl of non sugary cereal with skimmed milk. A low fat fruit yogurt. A glass of tomato juice.

Lunch **Creamy turkey salad:** mix cooked, chopped new potatoes with cooked turkey, basil leaves, chopped red onion, 2 tbsp 0% fat Greek yogurt and 1 tsp balsamic vinegar. Serve with mixed salad leaves and cherry tomatoes. A banana.

Dinner **Steak with couscous:** cook couscous according to packet instructions. Mix with 1 tbsp each of chopped fresh mint and parsley, juice of $^1/_2$ a lemon, 2 tsp olive oil, 1 chopped spring onion, 1 chopped tomato, diced cucumber and seasoning. Serve with grilled rump steak, seasoned with a little cayenne pepper and a kebab made with mushrooms, peppers and courgettes.

Y *Dessert* **Blackberry meringues:** (see recipe).

Calcium guidelines Add 150 ml (5 fl oz) skimmed milk to this menu plan to keep your daily calcium intake at the recommended levels (see p. 80 of your Eat Wisely book).

the *POINTS* Plan
menu plans

On the *POINTS* **Plan** you control calories with the *POINTS* system. **Eat any food, as long as you keep track** and watch your portions. The *POINTS* **Plan** chapter is full of delicious menu plans and recipes, all nutritionally balanced, giving you **variety and flexibility** to help you lose and maintain your weight.

Black Forest trifle, page 84

Weekend breakfast treat

total for the day

Breakfast **1 Apricot turnover:** (see recipe) served with a small glass (100 ml/3^1/$_2$ fl oz) of orange juice.

Lunch **Lazy lunch:** choose a ready made salad with a **POINTS** value of 4. Serve with 2 pineapple rings in natural juice.

Dinner **Chicken mustard parcels:** on a large square of foil, lay 50 g (1^3/$_4$ oz) of each of the following: finely shredded carrot, leek and courgette. Top with a 175 g (6 oz) skinless boneless chicken breast and drizzle over 1 tsp honey and 1 tsp wholegrain mustard. Fold the foil around like a Cornish pasty, leaving a gap at the top. Pour in 2 tbsp white wine and seal the foil. Bake in a preheated oven at 180°C for 35–40 minutes until cooked. Serve with 50 g (1^3/$_4$ oz) diced potatoes roasted with low fat cooking spray, along with 75 g (2^3/$_4$ oz) cooked peas and some asparagus.

Dessert **Chocolate mousse:** 1 small pot of ready made low fat chocolate mousse and 160 g (5^3/$_4$ oz) raspberries.

Snacks Use 300 ml (10 fl oz) skimmed milk throughout the day. A 150 g pot of virtually fat free plain yogurt.

Apricot turnovers

Takes 20 minutes to prepare, 20 minutes to cook *Makes 4*

24 POINTS *values per recipe*

340 calories *per serving*

1 x 240 g packet of croissant dough

4 dried ready to eat apricots (approximately 27 g)

4 teaspoons Weight Watchers Apricot Spread

2 teaspoons icing sugar

1 Preheat the oven to Gas Mark 4/180°C/fan oven160°C. Unroll the croissant dough and fold it in half. Roll out the dough on a piece of non stick baking parchment until it measures 60 cm x 15 cm (24 inches x 6 inches).

2 Cut into four squares. Take one square and fold in half diagonally to form a triangle. Starting 1 cm (^{1}/$_2$ inch) in at the folded side, cut a 1 cm (^{1}/$_2$ inch) wide border along the open sides. Leave 1 cm (^{1}/$_2$ inch) uncut at the end so the strips remain attached.

3 Unfold the triangle and lift the border strips up and slip one strip under the other. Pull across the base to the opposite corner and press the attached points of the strips to the corners of the base to seal. Put one dried apricot into the centre and transfer to a baking tray. Repeat to make three more.

4 Bake in the oven for 15–20 minutes until golden and cooked. Meanwhile, melt the apricot spread in a small pan and once the turnovers are cooked and still warm, drizzle each with 1 teaspoon of the spread over the dried apricot. Leave to cool and dust with icing sugar.

6 POINTS VALUE

Orange raspberry bites

Takes 10 minutes to prepare, 35 minutes to cook + cooling

Makes 6

22 POINTS *values per recipe*

160 calories *per serving*

zest of 1 orange

2 teaspoons cornflour

250 g (9 oz) ricotta

3 eggs *beaten*

75 g (2³/₄ oz) golden caster sugar

50 g (1³/₄ oz) fresh raspberries

❶ Preheat the oven to Gas Mark 3/160°C/fan oven 140°C and line a six hole non stick muffin tin with muffin cases. In a bowl, whisk together the orange zest, cornflour, ricotta, eggs and sugar until smooth.

❷ Divide the mixture between the muffin cases and top each with two or three raspberries in the centre. Bake in the oven for 30–35 minutes until golden and set.

❸ Leave to cool in the tin, then remove and serve.

Treat yourself

total for the day

4½ **Y** *Breakfast* **1 Orange raspberry bite:** (see recipe) served with a small glass (100 ml/3½ fl oz) of cranberry juice.

4 *Lunch* **Smoked salmon roll:** a 50 g (1³/₄ oz) roll, 50 g (1³/₄ oz) smoked salmon, 15 g (½ oz) low fat soft cheese and rocket. 1 kiwi fruit.

7 *Dinner* **Potato gratin with lamb:** put 100 g (3½ oz) grated potato and 1 grated onion in the base of an ovenproof dish and spray with low fat cooking spray. Bake in a preheated oven at 190°C for 30–35 minutes. Serve with a 125 g (4½ oz) grilled lamb chop, courgettes, cabbage and carrots.

2 *Dessert* **Fruit jelly:** serve sugar free raspberry jelly with a 210 g small can of mandarins in natural juice and a 60 g (2 oz) scoop of low fat vanilla ice cream.

2½ *Snacks* Use 600 ml (1 pint) skimmed milk throughout the day. A tube of Weight Watchers Fruities.

Fruity couscous

5¹/₂ POINTS *values per recipe*

340 calories *per serving*

150 ml (5 fl oz) fresh orange juice

60 g (2 oz) dried couscous

1 eating apple *cored and grated*

50 g (1³/₄ oz) fresh raspberries

¹/₂ tablespoon pumpkin seeds

¹/₂ tablespoon sunflower seeds

❶ Put the orange juice in a small lidded pan and bring to the boil. Add the couscous. Remove from the heat and cover.

❷ Leave for 5–7 minutes until swollen and most of the liquid has been absorbed.

❸ Stir in the grated apple and spoon into a bowl. Scatter over the raspberries and seeds and serve.

Fruit and spice

total for the day

Breakfast **Fruity couscous:** (see recipe).

Lunch **Cheesy hoops on toast:** a 200 g can of spaghetti hoops in tomato sauce on a toasted medium slice of wholemeal bread with 1 tbsp grated Parmesan. A pear.

Dinner **Quick vegetable curry:** cook ¹/₂ a diced onion and 1 crushed garlic clove in a non stick pan sprayed with low fat cooking spray for 4 minutes. Add 1 tbsp mild curry powder, 75 g (2³/₄ oz) small cauliflower florets, 1 tbsp tomato purée, 75 g (2³/₄ oz) frozen mixed vegetables, 300 ml (10 fl oz) vegetable stock and a 200 g can of chopped tomatoes. Bring to the boil, cover and simmer for 10 minutes. Stir in 1 tbsp chopped fresh coriander and serve with ¹/₂ a medium (70 g) naan bread.

Dessert **Fruity chocolate pot:** 50 g (1³/₄ oz) blueberries stirred into a 150 g pot of low fat chocolate mousse.

Snacks 300 ml (10 fl oz) skimmed milk used throughout the day. A 150 g pot low fat plain yogurt.

Lazy morning

total for the day

(**7** POINTS) *Breakfast* **Baked egg bun:** (see recipe) served with a skinny latte made with 300 ml (10 fl oz) skimmed milk.

(**4** POINTS) *Lunch* **Chicken Caesar salad:** put two slices of Parma Ham and two slices (30 g/1$^1/_4$ oz) of cooked chicken on a plate. Scatter over $^1/_2$ tbsp rinsed capers and top with lamb's lettuce, diced tomato and cucumber. Drizzle with 1 tbsp low fat Caesar dressing. 150 g (5$^1/_2$ oz) strawberries.

(**4$\frac{1}{2}$** POINTS) *Dinner* **Mediterranean style lamb:** marinate 100 g (3$^1/_2$ oz) lean lamb leg steak in a mixture of 10 drained and finely chopped, pitted olives in brine, 1 tbsp chopped mint, 1 tbsp chopped parsley, zest of $^1/_2$ a lemon and 1 crushed garlic clove. Spray the lamb with low fat cooking spray, grill to your liking and serve with 150 g (5$^1/_2$ oz) roasted sweet potato, broccoli and mange tout.

(**3$\frac{1}{2}$** POINTS) Ⓥ *Dessert* **Custard:** mix a 150 g pot of ready to serve low fat custard with 1 tbsp low fat soft cheese and 1 tsp rosewater. Chill until needed and serve with 2 tangerines and 50 g (1$^3/_4$ oz) blueberries.

(**1** POINTS) *Snacks* Use 150 ml (5 fl oz) skimmed milk throughout the day. 1 small glass (100 ml/3$^1/_2$ fl oz) of apple juice.

Baked egg buns

(**6** POINTS VALUE)

Takes 35 minutes *Serves 2*

12$^1/_2$ *POINTS* values per recipe

310 calories per serving

2 x 50 g (1$^3/_4$ oz) soft bread rolls

2 tablespoons roasted vegetable chutney

4 mini pork cocktail sausages

2 eggs

freshly ground black pepper

1 tablespoon fresh snipped chives *to garnish*

❶ Preheat the oven to Gas Mark 4/180°C/fan oven 160°C. Use an 8 cm (3$^1/_4$ inch) round cutter to cut a circle, 2 cm ($^3/_4$ inch) deep from the top of each roll. Remove and discard. Squidge the bread inside the roll to the sides to leave a large well in the centre of each.

❷ Spread 1 tablespoon chutney in the base of each well and top each with two sausages. Wrap both rolls in foil and put on a baking tray. Bake in the oven for 10 minutes.

❸ Remove the foil and crack 1 egg into each hole, on top of the sausages. Return to the oven and bake for 15–20 minutes until the eggs are just set. Season with freshly ground black pepper, sprinkle with chives and serve.

Ⓥ **Vegetarian tip:** simply replace the pork cocktail sausages with 2 chopped Quorn sausages in step 2 for a ***POINTS*** value of 5$^1/_2$ per serving.

Fruit and nut squares

Takes 10 minutes to prepare, 20 minutes to cook + 10 minutes cooling *Makes 9*

21^1/$_2$ POINTS *values per recipe*

155 calories *per serving*

^{1}/$_2$ x 170 g packet of dried berries and cherries

100 g (3^1/$_2$ oz) rolled oats

15 g (^{1}/$_2$ oz) cornflakes

1 tablespoon chopped toasted hazelnuts

1 tablespoon pumpkin seeds

50 g (1^3/$_4$ oz) dark brown sugar

2 tablespoons golden syrup

50 g (1^3/$_4$ oz) low fat polyunsaturated margarine

1. Preheat the oven to Gas Mark 5/190°C/fan oven 170°C. Line an 18 cm (7 inch) square baking tin with greaseproof paper. Put the dried berries and cherries, oats, cornflakes, hazelnuts and pumpkin seeds into a large bowl.
2. Put the sugar, syrup and polyunsaturated margarine into a pan and gently heat until the sugar has dissolved and the margarine is melted. Pour into the dry mixture and stir to coat everything in the syrup.
3. Spoon into the tin and level with the back of a spoon, pressing down to compact the mixture. Bake in the oven for 15–20 minutes until golden. Remove and leave to cool for 10 minutes. Remove from the tin and cut into nine squares. Leave to go cold, discard the paper and store in an air tight container.

Bake ahead

total for the d

(4^1/$_2$) *Breakfast* **1 Fruit and nut square:** (see recipe). A 100 g pot of low fat fromage frais.

(6^1/$_2$) *Lunch* **Beef roll:** spread a 50 g roll with 1 tbsp reduced fat mayonnaise, mixed with 1 tsp horseradish sauce. Fill with a 50 g (1^3/$_4$ oz) slice of cooked roast beef, lots of watercress and sliced tomatoes. A 50 g packet of ready to eat semi dried apricots.

(5) *Dinner* **Indian pork shashlic:** marinate 150 g (5^1/$_2$ oz) cubed lean pork tenderloin in 1 tbsp low fat yogurt mixed with 2 tsp Tandoori spice mix. Thread on to skewers with ^{1}/$_2$ a deseeded and diced red pepper and 1 quartered small onion. Grill for 10–15 minutes until cooked. Serve with a cucumber and tomato salad and 75 g (2^3/$_4$ oz) cooked rice.

(2^1/$_2$) *Dessert* **Mango and lime delight:** add the zest and juice of 1 lime to a drained 210 g can of mango in natural juice. Serve with 1 tbsp low fat crème fraîche.

(1^1/$_2$) *Snacks* Use 300 ml (10 fl oz) skimmed milk throughout the day. 1 apple.

Pastrami and ricotta pasta

Takes 25 minutes *Serves 2*

9¹/₂ POINTS *values per recipe*

250 calories *per serving*

80 g (3 oz) dried fusilli pasta

75 g (2³/₄ oz) ricotta cheese

10 pitted black olives in brine *sliced*

50 g (1³/₄ oz) cherry tomatoes *halved*

4 x 10 g (¹/₄ oz) slices of pastrami *chopped roughly*

50 g bag of wild rocket *chopped*

salt and freshly ground black pepper

❶ Cook the pasta in a large saucepan of boiling water for 12–15 minutes or according to packet instructions until 'al dente'. Drain and rinse in cold water until cold. Empty into a bowl.

❷ Stir through the ricotta, olives, tomatoes, pastrami and rocket. Check the seasoning and serve.

Ⓥ **Vegetarian tip:** replace the pastrami with the same quantity of vegetarian ham for a **POINTS** value of 4¹/₂ per serving.

Quick pasta for two

total for the day

② Ⓥ *Breakfast* A 30 g (1¹/₄ oz) bowl of branflakes with 150 ml (5 fl oz) skimmed milk.

⑤ *Lunch* **Pastrami and ricotta pasta:** (see recipe) served with a zero **POINTS** value salad.

⑦ *Dinner* **Baked cheesy turkey:** flatten 125 g (4¹/₂ oz) turkey steak between 2 sheets of cling film, with the end of a rolling pin until thin. Put 25 g (1 oz) reduced fat Brie and 25 g (1 oz) sliced mild pepperdew peppers on top of the steak. Place on top of 2 slices of Parma ham and roll up. Spray with low fat cooking spray and bake in a preheated oven at 190°C for 30 minutes until cooked. Serve with a 225 g (8 oz) jacket potato and a green salad.

③½ Ⓥ *Dessert* **Brioche with cherries:** top a 25 g (1 oz) slice of toasted brioche with 75 g (2³/₄ oz) warm pitted cherries in a light syrup and a 60 g (2 oz) scoop of low fat vanilla ice cream.

②½ *Snacks* Use 150 ml (5 fl oz) skimmed milk throughout the day. A 100 g pot of very low fat fromage frais. 25 g air popped popcorn.

Eastern feast

20 POINTS VALUE

total for the day

4½ POINTS ⓨ *Breakfast* **Sunrise smoothie:** whiz together 150 ml (5 fl oz) chilled orange juice (not concentrate) with 100 g (3½ oz) raspberries and a 150 g pot of very low fat plain yogurt in a blender until smooth. 1 toasted medium (90 g/3¼ oz) white or wholemeal muffin.

4 POINTS *Lunch* **3 Chinese prawn pancakes:** (see recipe) with any soup with a **POINTS** value of 1½ such as a 295 g can of Weight Watchers from Heinz Chicken Soup.

6 POINTS *Dinner* **Red Thai lamb noodles:** cook 40 g (1½ oz) medium egg noodles according to the packet instructions. Drain and rinse in cold water. Meanwhile, cut 100 g (3½ oz) lean lamb leg steak into thin strips and toss with 1 tbsp red Thai curry paste (or less, to taste) to coat. Heat a wok until hot and spray with low fat cooking spray. Stir fry the lamb for 2 minutes, stirring constantly. Add ½ a 300 g packet of mixed stir fry vegetables and 2 tbsp boiling water. Stir fry for 3–5 minutes. Toss through the cooked noodles and serve with a lime wedge.

2 POINTS ⓨ *Dessert* **Quick fruity nests:** defrost 75 g (2¾ oz) frozen summer fruits and whiz half in a food processor until puréed. Spoon into the centre of a 15 g (½ oz) ready made meringue nest, top with 1 tbsp low fat fruit fromage frais and the remaining defrosted fruit.

3½ POINTS *Snacks* Use 300 ml (10 fl oz) skimmed milk throughout the day. A 25 g bag of prawn crackers.

Chinese prawn pancakes

2½ POINTS VALUE

Takes 30 minutes *Serves 4*

9 *POINTS* *values per recipe*
165 calories *per serving*

250 g (9 oz) cooked and peeled tiger prawns
125 g (4½ oz) beansprouts
1 carrot *peeled and grated*
75 g (2¾ oz) cucumber *diced finely*
50 g (1¾ oz) radish *trimmed and grated*
½ x 25 g packet of fresh coriander *chopped roughly*
½ x 25 g packet of fresh mint *chopped roughly*
1 teaspoon caster sugar
1 tablespoon light soy sauce
juice of 2 limes
2 tablespoons sweet chilli sauce
1 teaspoon Thai fish sauce
12 Chinese pancakes
lime wedges *to serve*

❶ Put the prawns, beansprouts, carrot, cucumber, radish, coriander and mint in a large bowl.

❷ In another small bowl, whisk together the sugar, soy sauce, lime juice, chilli sauce and fish sauce.

❸ Pour the dressing over the prawn salad and toss to coat thoroughly.

❹ Put one pancake on a board and put a generous spoonful of the prawn salad in the centre. Roll up and place seam side down on a serving plate. Repeat with the remaining pancakes and prawn salad. Serve three pancakes each immediately, with lime wedges on the side.

Curried parsnip soup

Takes 25 minutes to prepare, 30 minutes to cook *Serves 6*

Y *vegan* ❋

8 POINTS *values per recipe*

115 calories *per serving*

low fat cooking spray

1 onion *chopped roughly*

2 garlic cloves *chopped*

1 tablespoon coriander seeds *crushed*

1 teaspoon mild curry powder

1 carrot *peeled and chopped*

750 g (1 lb 10 oz) parsnips *peeled and cut into chunks*

1 litre (1³/₄ pints) vegetable stock

1 medium glass (175 ml/6 fl oz) of low alcohol white wine

salt and freshly ground black pepper

chopped fresh coriander *to garnish*

1 Heat a large saucepan and spray with low fat cooking spray. Cook the onion and garlic for 3–4 minutes until softened. Add the coriander seeds and curry powder and cook for 1 minute.

2 Add the carrot, parsnips, vegetable stock and white wine. Bring to the boil. Reduced the heat and simmer for 30 minutes or until the vegetables are tender. Leave to cool slightly.

3 Then carefully whiz the soup in a blender or food processor until smooth. Return to the pan, season and gently warm through. Serve with coriander to garnish.

Simply delicious

total for the d

(2½) **Y** *Breakfast* A 30 g (1¹/₄ oz) bowl of cornflakes with 150 ml (5 fl oz) skimmed milk. 1 small glass (100 ml/3¹/₂ fl oz) of grapefruit juice.

(9) **Y** *Lunch* **Curried parsnip soup:** (see recipe) served with 50 g (1³/₄ oz) bag of vegetable crisps and a 50 g (1³/₄ oz) roll. 1 small banana. A 150 g pot of 0% fat Greek yogurt.

(4½) *Dinner* **Cod with pesto:** spread a 110 g (4 oz) skinless smoked cod fillet with 1 tbsp green pesto. Top with 1 tbsp breadcrumbs and bake in a preheated oven at 190°C for 10–15 minutes until golden. Serve with 100 g (3¹/₂ oz) boiled potatoes, baby corn and 1 tbsp broad beans.

(3½) **Y** *Dessert* **Rice pudding with apricots:** serve ¹/₂ x 425 g can of Weight Watchers Rice Pudding with a 227 g can of apricot halves in juice.

(½) *Snacks* Use 150 ml (5 fl oz) skimmed milk throughout the day.

Fruity chicken salad

Takes 20 minutes to prepare *Serves 2*

6 POINTS *values per recipe*
195 calories *per serving*

1 orange
200 g (7 oz) fennel bulb *trimmed and sliced finely*
2 spring onions *sliced finely*
25 g packet of fresh flat leaf parsley *chopped roughly*
50 g (1³/₄ oz) light feta cheese *crumbled*
4 x 30 g (1¹/₄ oz) slices of cooked chicken
¹/₂ pomegranate *seeds reserved and pith discarded*
salt and freshly ground black pepper

1 Using a knife, carefully cut away the top and bottom of the orange. Stand the orange upright and then cut away the peel and pith, in a downward motion. Cut between the membranes to remove the segments. (Do this over a jug to catch the juice). Put the segments into a bowl.

2 Add the fennel, spring onions, parsley leaves and half the cheese. Pour the orange juice over the salad and gently toss to coat. Season.

3 Divide the chicken between the plates and top with the fennel salad. Scatter over the pomegranate seeds and remaining cheese.

(3) POINTS VALUE

Refreshingly good

(20) POINTS VALUE total for the day

(5) POINTS **Ⓨ** *Breakfast* **Eggs Benedict:** top a toasted 90 g (3 oz) muffin with 1 poached egg and 1 tbsp ready made hollandaise sauce.

(4) POINTS *Lunch* **Fruity chicken salad:** (see recipe) served with a 30 g (1¹/₄ oz) mini toasted pitta bread.

(5½) POINTS **Ⓨ** *Dinner* **Eastern stir fry:** heat a wok until hot and spray with low fat cooking spray. Stir fry 300 g (10¹/₂ oz) mixed stir fry vegetables for 5 minutes. Add 1 tsp Chinese five spice powder, 2 tbsp soy sauce and 1 tbsp chopped coriander. Serve with 150 g (5¹/₂ oz) cooked rice sprinkled with 1 tbsp chopped peanuts.

(3½) POINTS **Ⓨ** *Dessert* **Apricot tart:** cut an 8 cm (3¹/₄ inches) square (weighing 30 g/1¹/₄ oz) of ready rolled puff pastry. Roll lightly to measure 10 cm (4 inches). Put 4 apricot halves, drained from juice, cut side down, on the square. Drizzle with ¹/₂ tsp honey. Bake at 200°C for 15 minutes. Drizzle with another ¹/₂ tsp honey.

(2) POINTS *Snacks* Use 300 ml (10 fl oz) skimmed milk throughout the day. 150 g pot of very low fat plain yogurt.

Easy vegetarian

(3½) **(Y)** *Breakfast* 2 Weetabix topped with 50 g (1³/₄ oz) raspberries, 50 g (1³/₄ oz) blueberries and 150 ml (5 fl oz) skimmed milk. 1 small glass (100 ml/3¹/₂ fl oz) of orange juice.

(5) *Lunch* A ready made salad with a *POINTS* value of 4, 10 black olives in brine, drained and 2 satsumas.

(7½) **(Y)** *Dinner* **Baked red pepper crumble:** (see recipe) served with a green salad.

(1½) **(Y)** *Dessert* **Ice cream treat:** a 60 g (2 oz) scoop of low fat vanilla ice cream with 1 ice cream wafer and 1 tbsp of 'hundred and thousands'.

(2½) *Snacks* Use 450 ml (16 fl oz) skimmed milk throughout the day. 100 g (3¹/₂ oz) portion of cherries with 1 tbsp low fat plain yogurt.

Baked red pepper crumble

Takes 20 minutes to prepare, 25 minutes to cook *Serves 4*

(Y)

29¹/₂ *POINTS* values per recipe
325 calories per serving

400 g (14 oz) fresh penne pasta
700 g jar of passata with onion and garlic
12 black olives in brine *drained*
4 spring onions *sliced finely*
10 fresh basil leaves *shredded*
200 g (7 oz) roasted red peppers in brine *drained and sliced finely*
75 g (2³/₄ oz) dolcelatte cheese *crumbled*
2 tablespoons grated Parmesan
¹/₂ medium slice of white bread *diced finely*
low fat cooking spray
salt and freshly ground black pepper

① Preheat the oven to Gas Mark 4/180°C/fan oven 160°C. Bring a large saucepan of water to the boil and blanch the penne for 1 minute. Drain, reserving 100 ml (3¹/₂ fl oz) cooking water and return both the penne and reserved liquid to the pan.

② Stir in the passata, olives, spring onions and basil leaves. Season. Spoon into a 1 litre (1³/₄ pints) ovenproof dish. Scatter over the peppers, crumble over the dolcelatte cheese and top with 1 tablespoon of the Parmesan and the bread cubes.

③ Spray with low fat cooking spray and bake in the oven for 25 minutes until golden and the pasta is cooked. Sprinkle with the remaining Parmesan and serve.

Chargrilled turkey steaks with korma rice

Takes 45 minutes *Serves 2*

13 *POINTS* values per recipe

495 calories per serving

2 x 100 g (3^1/$_2$ oz) turkey steaks

zest and juice of 1 lime

low fat cooking spray

1 onion *chopped finely*

1 heaped teaspoon Korma spice blend

100 g (3^1/$_2$ oz) long grain rice

125 ml (4 fl oz) Chinese cooking wine

250 ml (9 fl oz) vegetable stock

2 eggs

30 g (1^1/$_4$ oz) raisins

150 g (5^1/$_2$ oz) baby spinach *rinsed*

salt and freshly ground black pepper

1 Put the turkey steaks into a shallow non metallic dish and coat in the lime zest and juice. Set aside.

2 Heat a wide, lidded, non stick pan. Spray with low fat cooking spray. Cook the onion for 3–4 minutes until softened. Stir in the korma spices, rice and cooking wine. Bubble rapidly for 1 minute. Add the stock. Bring to the boil. Cover and simmer for 12–15 minutes until tender.

3 Meanwhile, put the eggs into a pan of cold water and bring to the boil. Simmer for 5 minutes and then plunge into cold water. Set aside.

4 When the rice is cooked, stir in the raisins and spinach, cover and keep on a low heat, stirring from time to time until the spinach is wilted. Season. Meanwhile, heat a griddle or non stick frying pan until hot. Spray the turkey steaks with low fat cooking spray and cook the steaks for 10 minutes, turning halfway until cooked.

5 Peel and halve the eggs. Serve the rice with the turkey steaks, putting the eggs on the side.

Indian summer

total for the

2^1/$_2$ **Y** *Breakfast* A 30 g (1^1/$_4$ oz) bowl of muesli with 150 ml (5 fl oz) warm skimmed milk topped with 50 g (1^3/$_4$ oz) each of raspberries and blackberries.

6^1/$_2$ *Lunch* **Soup with cheese toastie:** any soup with a ***POINTS*** value of 1^1/$_2$ such as a 300 g can of Weight Watchers from Heinz Carrot and Lentil Soup. Spread 2 medium slices of wholemeal bread each with 1 tsp margarine. Sandwich with 30 g (1^3/$_4$ oz) ham and 25 g (1 oz) grated half fat Cheddar. Toast under the grill, turning once until the cheese has melted.

6^1/$_2$ *Dinner* **Chargrilled turkey steaks with korma rice.** (see recipe) served with a large salad of mixed leaves, tomatoes and cucumber.

3 **Y** *Dessert* **Strawberry delight:** mix 75 g (2^3/$_4$ oz) very finely chopped strawberries with 1 tbsp Quark and the juice of ^{1}/$_2$ an orange. Scoop up with 2 Weight Watchers Lemon and Ginger Cookies.

1^1/$_2$ *Snacks* Use 450 ml (16 fl oz) skimmed milk throughout the day.

Vegetarian shepherd's pie

Takes 40 minutes to prepare, 45 minutes to cook *Serves 4*

 ❄

16¹/₂ *POINTS* values per recipe

340 calories per serving

500 g (1 lb 2 oz) sweet potato *cut into even chunks*

low fat cooking spray

1 onion *chopped finely*

2 garlic cloves *crushed*

1 celery stick *diced finely*

1 carrot *diced finely*

1 tablespoon chopped fresh rosemary leaves

125 ml (4 fl oz) red wine

350 g packet of Quorn mince

1 tablespoon plain flour

700 g jar of passata

220 g can of butter beans *drained and rinsed*

25 g (1 oz) reduced fat Cheddar cheese *grated*

salt and freshly ground black pepper

1 Put the sweet potato into a lidded pan and cover with cold water. Bring to the boil, cover and simmer for 20 minutes. Drain, mash and season.

2 Meanwhile, preheat the oven to Gas Mark 5/190°C/fan oven 170°C. Heat a non stick saucepan. Spray with low fat cooking spray. Gently fry the onion, garlic, celery, carrot and rosemary for 5–8 minutes until beginning to soften. Add the red wine. Bubble for 2 minutes to reduce.

3 Stir in the Quorn mince and flour. Pour in the passata and cook for 5 minutes. Stir through the butter beans, check seasoning and transfer to a 1 litre (1³/₄ pint) ovenproof dish.

4 Top the Quorn mince with the mash, spreading evenly with a fork. Sprinkle over the cheese and bake in the oven for 40–45 minutes until golden and bubbling.

Veggie family favourite

20 POINTS VALUE total for the day

5½ Ⓨ *Breakfast* **Fruit compote:** soak 15 g (¹/₂ oz) dried prunes, 50 g (1³/₄ oz) dried apricots, 1 dried fig, 4 dried apple rings, 1 green tea bag and a pared strip of orange zest in 150 ml (5 fl oz) boiling water for 30 minutes. Serve with 1 tbsp 0% fat Greek yogurt. 1 toasted crumpet spread with 1 tsp low fat spread and 1 tsp Weight Watchers fruit spread.

5 Ⓨ *Lunch* **Houmous with pitta:** 60 g (2 oz) reduced fat houmous, 60 g (2 oz) pitta bread. A mixed salad with 1 tbsp fat free salad dressing. A peach.

4½ Ⓨ *Dinner* **Vegetarian shepherd's pie:** (see recipe) served with spinach, baby carrots, 1 heaped tbsp peas.

3 Ⓨ *Dessert* **Poached pears:** poach 1 peeled, cored and halved medium pear in 150 ml (5 fl oz) water, 1 tbsp caster sugar and 1 tsp vanilla essence in a pan for 10–15 minutes. A 100 g pot of very low fat fruit fromage frais.

2 *Snacks* Use 300 ml (10 fl oz) skimmed milk throughout the day. A 175 ml glass of low alcohol wine. 3 apricots.

total for the day

(2½) (Y) *Breakfast* **Banana split:** slice 1 banana in half lengthways. Put in a dish and spoon over 1 tbsp Quark. Drizzle with 2 tsp maple syrup.

(6½) *Lunch* **Sardine sandwich:** top 2 toasted 30 g (1¼ oz) slices of French baguette with a 120 g can of sardines in tomato sauce. Serve with herb salad, diced tomato and sliced red onion salsa. A 150 g pot of very low fat plain yogurt.

(8) *Dinner* **Winter pork ragu:** (see recipe) served with 150 g (5½ oz) cooked couscous, green beans and tender stem broccoli.

(1½) *Dessert* **Chocolate mousse:** a 65 g pot of low fat chocolate mousse.

(1½) *Snacks* Use 300 ml (10 fl oz) skimmed milk throughout the day. 100 g (3½ oz) raspberries.

Winter pork ragu

Takes 30 minutes to prepare, 40 minutes to cook *Serves 4*

22½ *POINTS* values per recipe

305 calories per serving

low fat cooking spray

500 g (1 lb 2 oz) lean pork tenderloin *cut into 2 cm (¾ inch) cubes*

1 onion *chopped finely*

1 teaspoon ground cinnamon

¼ teaspoon grated nutmeg

1 star anise

1 tablespoon plain flour

1 red chilli *deseeded and chopped finely*

2 cm (¾ inch) piece of fresh ginger *peeled and grated*

25 g (1 oz) whole blanched almonds

600 ml (1 pint) vegetable stock

1 tablespoon tomato purée

100 ml (3½ fl oz) reduced fat coconut milk

50 g (1¾ oz) ready to eat dried apricots *halved*

salt and freshly ground black pepper

25 g packet of fresh coriander *chopped roughly, to serve*

1 Heat a large, lidded heavy based saucepan and spray with low fat cooking spray. Add the pork in batches and cook for 1 minute on each side until brown. Transfer to a plate and set aside.

2 Spray the pan again with low fat cooking spray and gently cook the onion for 3–4 minutes until softened. Add the cinnamon, nutmeg, star anise, plain flour, chilli, ginger, almonds and return the pork to the saucepan. Cook for 2 minutes stirring constantly.

3 Pour in the vegetable stock, tomato purée and coconut milk. Bring to the boil, cover and simmer for 35 minutes, stirring from time to time. Stir in the apricots and cook gently for 5 minutes. Check the seasoning, stir in the coriander and serve.

Salmon strudel

Takes 25 minutes to prepare, 40 minutes to cook + 20 minutes
to cool *Serves 4*

18¹/₂ POINTS values per recipe
320 calories per serving

1 courgette *trimmed and sliced*

2 red peppers *quartered and deseeded*

1 red onion *cut into thin wedges*

2 tablespoons balsamic vinegar

low fat cooking spray

8 x 14 g sheets of filo pastry (30 cm x 30 cm/12 inches x 12 inches)

3 x 125 g (4¹/₂ oz) salmon fillets *cut in half horizontally to make 6 thin fillets*

2 tablespoons low fat garlic and herb soft cheese

salt and freshly ground black pepper

① Preheat the oven to Gas Mark 6/200°C/fan oven 180°C. Put the courgette slices, peppers and onions on to a baking tray, drizzle with balsamic vinegar and spray with low fat cooking spray. Season and roast in the oven for 20 minutes until starting to char a little. Leave to cool for 20 minutes.

② Lay two sheets of filo pastry on a non stick baking tray slightly overlapping to make a square. Spray with low fat cooking spray and lay another 2 sheets over. Repeat this once more.

③ Lay the thin salmon fillets down the centre of the square leaving a 2.5 cm (1 inch) border at either end. Season with freshly ground black pepper and then spread the soft cheese over the fillets. Arrange the cooled vegetables on top.

④ Spray the exposed filo pastry with low fat cooking spray and fold the pastry up and over to enclose the salmon completely, sealing the ends. Spray with low fat cooking spray and crumple the remaining filo sheets over the top. Spray once more with low fat cooking spray and bake in the oven for 20 minutes until golden and cooked.

Three course dinner

total for the

3¹/₂ Ⓨ *Breakfast* A 30 g (1¹/₄ oz) bowl of cereal with 150 ml (5 fl oz) skimmed milk, 10 g (¹/₄ oz) dried cranberries. 1 small banana.

4¹/₂ *Lunch* **Beef salad:** toss diced beetroot, sliced radish, salad leaves, 30 g (1¹/₄ oz) lean cooked beef and 1 tbsp low fat dressing. A 50 g (1³/₄ oz) bread roll. 2 figs.

1¹/₂ Ⓨ *Dinner Starter* **Roast tomatoes:** (serves 4) whiz 1 medium bread slice, 1 garlic clove, 1 tbsp capers. Use to top 4 halved tomatoes. Roast at 200°C for 10 minutes.

5¹/₂ *Main* **Salmon strudel:** (see recipe) served with 100 g (3¹/₂ oz) boiled new potatoes, mange tout and carrots.

1/₂ *Dessert* **Passion fruit pud:** (serves 4) dissolve 15 g (¹/₂ oz) sugar free orange jelly in 300 ml (10 fl oz) boiling water. Add 300 ml (10 fl oz) very low fat fromage frais. Chill for 3 hours. Top with the pulp of a passion fruit.

5¹/₂ *Snacks* Use 150 ml (5 fl oz) skimmed milk throughout the day. 175 ml (6 fl oz) glass of wine. 1 toasted crumpet with 2 tsp peanut butter.

Mini spicy nuggets

Takes 20 minutes to prepare, 15 minutes to cook *Serves 2*

 Y

7 *POINTS* *values per recipe*

255 calories *per serving*

140 g packet of Quorn tandoori pieces

1 egg *beaten*

1 red chilli *deseeded and chopped finely*

1 tablespoon snipped fresh chives

1 tablespoon chopped fresh coriander

30 g (1¹/₄ oz) frozen peas *defrosted*

1 medium slice of white bread *made into breadcrumbs*

low fat cooking spray

4 tablespoons sweet chilli sauce *to serve*

1 Preheat the oven to Gas Mark 6/200°C/fan oven 180°C and line a baking tray with non stick baking parchment.

2 Put the Quorn pieces into a food processor and whiz until finely minced. Transfer to a bowl.

3 Add the egg, chilli, chives, coriander, peas and breadcrumbs to the Quorn. Bring together to form a soft dough. Using wet hands, shape the mixture into six small nuggets.

4 Transfer to the baking tray, spray with low fat cooking spray and bake in the oven for 15 minutes until golden. Serve warm and dip into the chilli sauce.

Spicy dinner

 total for the day

(2) Y *Breakfast* **Cinnamon toast:** grill 2 halved, stoned plums for 5 minutes until starting to caramelize. Toast 1 medium slice of white bread and then spread with 1 tsp low fat polyunsaturated margarine mixed with ¹/₄ tsp ground cinnamon. Top with the plums.

(7) *Lunch* A ready made sandwich with a *POINTS* value of 6¹/₂, a large mixed salad with fat free dressing. A kiwi.

(5¹/₂) Y *Dinner* **Mini spicy nuggets:** (see recipe) served with 40 g (1¹/₂ oz) cooked egg noodles, tossed with 2 tbsp soy sauce. A coleslaw made from shredded red cabbage, fresh mint, fresh coriander and finely sliced onion tossed with ¹/₂ tsp wasabi and 1 tsp lime juice.

(4) *Dessert* **Banoffee pie:** put 30 g (1¹/₄ oz) finely chopped dried dates in a bowl. Pour over a 120 g Weight Watchers Toffee Yogurt. Top with 1 sliced small banana, 10 g (¹/₄ oz) grated plain chocolate. Freeze for 45 minutes.

(1¹/₂) *Snacks* Use 300 ml (10 fl oz) skimmed milk throughout the day. 1 tube of Weight Watchers Fruities.

Fire up the barbecue

total for the day

(2½) (Y) *Breakfast* A 30 g (1¼ oz) bowl of cereal with 150 ml (5 fl oz) skimmed milk. ½ a grapefruit.

(5¼) *Lunch* **Turkey sandwich:** grill 3 lean turkey rashers and sandwich between 2 slices of medium wholemeal bread with 1 tbsp reduced fat mayonnaise, a sliced tomato and some shredded lettuce. A 210 g can of apricots in natural juice with a pot of sugar free jelly.

(6¼) *Dinner* **Barbecued beef and prawns:** (see recipe) served with a large mixed salad drizzled with 1 tbsp light salad cream, 2 tbsp reduced calorie coleslaw, 1 medium slice of garlic bread.

(2½) (Y) *Dessert* **Fruit salad:** a mixed fruit salad made from 150 g (5½ oz) sliced strawberries, 1 peeled and segmented orange, 50 g (1¾ oz) grapes and a 60 g (2 oz) scoop of low fat ice cream.

(3) *Snacks* Use 300 ml (10 fl oz) skimmed milk throughout the day. A 150 g pot of low fat fruit yogurt.

Barbecued beef and prawns

Takes 45 minutes + 30 minutes marinating *Serves 4*

11 POINTS values per recipe
180 calories per serving

1 garlic clove *crushed*
1 teaspoon Dijon mustard
1 tablespoon chopped fresh rosemary
zest and juice of 1 lemon
2 tablespoons Pernod
250 g (9 oz) sirloin steak *cut into 1 cm (½ inch) strips*
125 g (4½ oz) raw, peeled tiger prawns
200 g (7 oz) miniature new potatoes
2 small red onions *halved*
low fat cooking spray
freshly ground black pepper

❶ In a bowl, mix together the garlic, mustard, rosemary, lemon zest and juice and Pernod. Season with freshly ground black pepper. Add the beef and prawns and turn to coat thoroughly. Leave to marinate for 30 minutes.

❷ Meanwhile, put the miniature potatoes in a lidded pan of cold water and bring to the boil. Cover and simmer for 5 minutes. Add onion halves and continue to simmer for a further 5 minutes. Drain and plunge into cold water to cool and then drain again.

❸ Cut the onions in half again to make eight wedges in total. Thread the potatoes, onion, beef and prawns on to four skewers, alternating them. Spray with low fat cooking spray and barbecue (or cook under a medium grill) for 10 minutes, turning until cooked. Serve immediately.

Pork schnitzel

Takes 20 minutes to prepare, 25 minutes to cook *Serves 4*

❋ *pork steak only*

19 POINTS *values per recipe*

430 calories *per serving*

4 x 150 g (5¹/₂ oz) lean pork loin steaks *visible fat removed*

2 medium slices of white bread

1 teaspoon paprika

1 egg *beaten*

1 tablespoon plain flour

low fat cooking spray

25 g packet of fresh flat leaf parsley *chopped finely*

2 garlic cloves *crushed*

2 teaspoons extra virgin olive oil

zest and juice of 1 small lemon

❶ Preheat the oven to Gas Mark 5/190°C/fan oven 170°C and put a baking tray in the oven to preheat. Put the pork steaks between two sheets of cling film and place on a board. With the end of the rolling pin, bash the pork to flatten until 1 cm (¹/₂ inch) thick. Set aside.

❷ In a food processor, whiz the bread and paprika to fine crumbs, then empty into a shallow dish. Put the egg into a separate shallow bowl. Dust the pork steaks lightly with the flour, shaking off the excess. One at a time, dip the pork steaks into the egg and then into the breadcrumbs, ensuring the whole steak is coated. Repeat with the remaining pork steaks.

❸ Remove the baking tray from the oven and then transfer the steaks to the preheated baking tray and spray with low fat cooking spray. Bake in the oven for 20–25 minutes until golden and the juices run clear.

❹ Meanwhile, in a small bowl mix together the parsley, garlic, oil, lemon zest and juice. Serve the pork schnitzel, topped with a generous spoonful of the parsley mixture.

Alpine day

total for the d...

④ Ⓨ *Breakfast* **Snowy porridge:** gently cook 30 g (1¹/₄ oz) rolled oats, 150 ml (5 fl oz) skimmed milk, 5 tbsp water and 20 g (³/₄ oz) raisins in a pan for 3–4 minutes. Serve with orange segments and ¹/₂ tbsp desiccated coconut.

⑤ *Lunch* **Grilled chicken and cheese:** grill a medium slice of bread, spread with ¹/₂ tsp wholegrain mustard and top with 30 g (1¹/₄ oz) wafer thin cooked chicken, 10 g (¹/₄ oz) grated Gruyère cheese and 1 sliced tomato. Grill again until melted. Serve with 2 tbsp mustard cress. A 100 g pot of low fat plain fromage frais and an apple.

⑥ *Dinner* **Pork schnitzel:** (see recipe) served with 125 g (4¹/₂ oz) cooked spaghetti and a large zero **POINTS** value mixed salad.

4¹/₂ Ⓨ *Dessert* **Custard fondue:** heat a 150 g pot of low fat custard then pour into a bowl. Dip in 25 g (1 oz) cubed Madeira cake and 150 g (5¹/₂ oz) strawberries.

¹/₂ *Snacks* Use 150 ml (5 fl oz) skimmed milk throughout the day.

Mediterranean meatballs

Takes 45 minutes to prepare, 30 minutes to cook *Serves 4*

20 POINTS values per recipe

260 calories per serving

500 g (1 lb 2 oz) extra lean beef mince

50 g (1³/₄ oz) dried lemon, parsley and thyme stuffing mix

1 egg *beaten*

low fat cooking spray

salt and freshly ground black pepper

For the tomato sauce

1 onion *sliced*

1 celery stick *diced finely*

1 carrot *peeled and diced finely*

¹/₂ red pepper *deseeded and diced finely*

1 garlic clove *crushed*

700 g jar of passata

250 ml (9 fl oz) vegetable stock

1 teaspoon dried oregano

1 teaspoon dried herbes de Provence

1 teaspoon Worcestershire sauce

2 tablespoons chopped fresh flat leaf parsley *to garnish*

❶ Mix together the mince, stuffing mix and egg until combined. Season. Using wet hands, shape the mixture into 20 golf ball sized balls.

❷ Heat a wide, non stick lidded pan and spray with low fat cooking spray. Gently fry the meatballs for 5 minutes, in batches if necessary, turning until brown. Remove and set aside.

❸ Heat the same pan again. Spray with low fat cooking spray. Cook the onion, celery, carrot, pepper and garlic, for 5–8 minutes until soft.

❹ Stir in the passata, stock, herbs and Worcestershire sauce. Return the meatballs to the pan and bring to the boil. Cover and simmer gently for 30 minutes until sauce has thickened. Garnish with parsley.

Family fiesta

Y *Breakfast* **Iced mocha:** mix 1 tbsp low fat drinking chocolate and 1 tsp instant coffee in 150 ml (5 fl oz) warm skimmed milk. Whiz with 100 ml (3¹/₂ fl oz) cold water, 1 tbsp oatmeal and ice cubes. 1 orange.

Y *Lunch* **Spicy dip:** whiz 3 tbsp canned mixed pulses with 150 g low fat plain yogurt, 1 tbsp low fat soft cheese, 1 tbsp lemon juice, 1 tsp Jerk seasoning. Serve with celery, sliced pepper, 1 mini pitta. 50 g (1³/₄ oz) grapes.

Dinner **Mediterranean meatballs:** (see recipe) served with 175 g (6 oz) cooked pasta and green beans.

Y *Dessert* **Meringue pots:** (serves 4) stew 1 apple, 3 small plums, 1 tbsp water, 1 tbsp caster sugar, covered, for 15 minutes. Whisk 1 egg white until foamy. Add 1 tbsp caster sugar and whisk until soft peaks. Divide fruit into 4 dishes, top each with 1 tbsp ready made low fat custard. Spread over some meringue. Grill until golden.

Snacks Use 150 ml (5 fl oz) skimmed milk throughout the day. 2 Jaffa Cakes.

Gastro pub food

3 POINTS **Y** *Breakfast* A 30 g (1¼ oz) bowl of All Bran with a 150 g pot of 0% fat Greek yogurt and 2 tbsp fruit compote.

6 POINTS *Lunch* **Ploughman's plate:** spread 2 slices of wholemeal bread with 1 tbsp pickle. Fill with 25 g (1 oz) grated reduced fat Cheddar, a medium slice (30 g/1¼ oz) of honey roast ham and ½ a cored and thinly sliced apple. The remaining ½ apple.

5½ POINTS *Dinner* **Huntsman chicken:** (see recipe) served with 150 g (5½ oz) potato, mashed with 1 tbsp skimmed milk, carrots, shredded spring greens and broccoli.

5 POINTS **Y** *Dessert* **Fruity tiramisu:** mix together 1 tsp instant coffee, 2 tbsp boiling water and 1 tbsp dry sherry. Dip 3 sponge fingers into the coffee mixture and put in the bottom of a dessert bowl. Mix together 2 tbsp Quark with 50 g (1¾ oz) raspberries and spoon on top of the sponge fingers. Dip 3 more sponge fingers in the remaining coffee mixture and lay on top of the Quark mixture. Chill until needed. To serve, grate 15 g (½ oz) chocolate over the tiramisu.

½ POINTS *Snacks* Use 150 ml (5 fl oz) skimmed milk throughout the day.

Huntsman chicken

Takes 20 minutes to prepare, 30 minutes to cook *Serves 4*

17 *POINTS* values per recipe

240 calories *per serving*

4 x 150 g (5½ oz) skinless boneless chicken breasts

4 rashers of lean back bacon

1 tablespoon finely chopped fresh flat leaf parsley

For the barbecue sauce

low fat cooking spray

20 silverskin onions *drained and rinsed*

1 garlic clove *crushed*

1 tablespoon light brown sugar

2 tablespoons cider vinegar

1 tablespoon tomato ketchup

2 teaspoons Dijon mustard

1 teaspoon mild chilli powder

1 tablespoon tomato purée

1 tablespoon brown sauce

1 Preheat the oven to Gas Mark 5/190°C/fan oven 170°C. To make the barbecue sauce, heat a saucepan and spray with low fat cooking spray. Cook the onions and garlic for 3–4 minutes until lightly browned. Add the remaining ingredients, 125 ml (4 fl oz) water and bring to the boil. Simmer for 5 minutes until beginning to thicken. Set aside.

2 Wrap each chicken breast with a rasher of bacon and put into an ovenproof dish. Pour over the BBQ sauce and bake in the oven for 30 minutes until cooked. Sprinkle with parsley and serve.

Y **Vegetarian tip:** wrap 4 Quorn chicken style fillets each in 1 Quorn style bacon rasher and cook with BBQ sauce in step 2, for a *POINTS* value of 1½ per serving.

Beef Wellington

Takes 30 minutes to prepare, 45 minutes to cook *Serves 4*

32^1/$_2$ *POINTS* values per recipe

430 calories *per serving*

25 g packet of dried mixed mushrooms

low fat cooking spray

1 red onion *chopped finely*

2 garlic cloves *crushed*

75 g (2^3/$_4$ oz) chestnut mushrooms *wiped and chopped finely*

1 tablespoon fresh thyme leaves

2 tablespoons low fat soft cheese

450 g (1 lb) lean beef fillet

200 g (7 oz) ready rolled puff pastry *cut into a 20 cm x 23 cm rectangle*

1 egg *beaten*

salt and freshly ground black pepper

1 Soak the dried mushrooms in enough boiling water to cover. Set aside. Meanwhile, heat a non stick frying pan and spray with low fat cooking spray. Cook the onion, garlic, chestnut mushrooms and 2 tablespoons of the mushroom soaking liquid for 10 minutes. Remove from the heat.

2 Drain the dried mushrooms, and chop finely. Stir into the cooked mushroom mixture with the thyme and soft cheese. Season and leave to go cold for about 10 minutes.

3 Meanwhile, heat a non stick frying pan until hot and spray with low fat cooking spray. Cook the beef for 1 minute on each side to brown. Remove and leave for 10 minutes.

4 Preheat the oven to Gas Mark 6/200°C/fan oven 180°C. Roll out the pastry to measure 23 cm x 25 cm. Put the beef fillet along one side leaving a 2.5 cm (1 inch) border and top with the mushroom mixture.

5 Brush around the beef with egg and fold over the pastry to enclose the beef. Seal the edges, trimming where necessary. Brush with the remaining egg. Bake in the oven for 40–45 minutes until cooked.

Stylish entertaining

total for the d

5 *Breakfast* **Fruit sundae:** layer in a glass a 100 g pot of Weight Watchers Black Forest Layered Fromage Frais, 40 g (1^1/$_2$ oz) granola and 50 g (1^3/$_4$ oz) fresh raspberries. A 300 ml (10 fl oz) skinny latte.

2^1/$_2$ *Vegan* **Y** *Lunch* **Zingy salad:** segment 1 pink grapefruit over a jug, reserving the juice. Mix with 75 g (2^3/$_4$ oz) blanched asparagus, 1 toasted and cubed 40 g (1^1/$_2$ oz) slice of ciabatta and a handful of salad leaves. Whisk reserved juice with 1 tsp mustard. Drizzle over.

1^1/$_2$ *Dinner Starter* **Salmon and salsa:** (serves 4) mix 1 diced papaya, zest and juice of 2 limes and 1 tbsp chopped dill. Season. Serve with 50 g (1^3/$_4$ oz) smoked salmon per person.

8 *Main* **Beef Wellington:** (see recipe) served with sugar snap peas and carrots.

3 **Y** *Dessert* **Mocha kisses:** (serves 4) mix 15 g (1/$_2$ oz) low fat margarine with 5 tbsp icing sugar, 1 tsp cocoa, 1 tsp hot water and 1 tsp instant coffee. Use to sandwich together 16 soft amaretti biscuits.

Belgian mussels

Takes 30 minutes *Serves 2*

7¹/₂ POINTS *values per recipe*
335 calories *per serving*

600 g (1lb 5 oz) fresh mussels

1 garlic clove *chopped*

100 ml (3¹/₂ fl oz) white wine

4 spring onions *sliced finely*

2 tablespoons double cream

1 tablespoon finely chopped fresh flat leaf parsley

1 tablespoon finely chopped fresh dill

salt and freshly ground black pepper

1   To clean the mussels, run them under cold water and pull off the beard (the feathery strands on the side). Tap any open mussels on a board, which should make them close. Don't use any that stay open.

2   Put the garlic, 100 ml (3¹/₂ fl oz) water and wine into a large lidded pan and bring to the boil. Cover and simmer for 5 minutes. Add the mussels and quickly replace the lid. Cook for 3–4 minutes, occasionally shaking the pan. Check that the mussels have opened. If not, cook for 1 minute more.

3   Remove the mussels and place in two large bowls, discarding any closed mussels and cover each bowl with foil to keep warm. Add the spring onions and double cream to the pan and bubble for a few minutes until thickened. Season. Remove foil and pour the cream sauce over the mussels and scatter with the parsley and dill to serve.

Gourmet seafood

total for the day

(3¹/₂) ⓨ *Breakfast* **Pepper and tomato eggs:** cook ¹/₂ a sliced onion, 1 deseeded and sliced red pepper and 75 g (2³/₄ oz) halved cherry tomatoes for 5 minutes. Crack in 1 egg, cover and cook for 5 minutes. 1 toasted medium slice of bread, spread with 1 tsp low fat polyunsaturated margarine. 1 orange.

(7) *Lunch* **Jacket potato:** 225 g (8 oz) jacket potato topped with 50 g (1³/₄ oz) cooked sliced mushrooms, mixed with 50 g (1³/₄ oz) diced cooked chicken and 1 tbsp reduced fat mayonnaise. A 150 g pot of 0% fat Greek yogurt. 225 g (8 oz) fresh strawberries.

(6) *Dinner* **Belgian mussels:** (see recipe) served with a 50 g (1³/₄ oz) bread roll and a mixed salad drizzled with balsamic vinegar.

(2) ⓨ *Dessert* **Afragato:** scoop 60 g (2 oz) low fat vanilla ice cream into a cup, pour over hot espresso coffee and grate over a 7 g square of milk chocolate.

(1¹/₂) *Snacks* Use 300 ml (10 fl oz) skimmed milk throughout the day. 100 g (3¹/₂ oz) fresh cherries.

Chinese comfort

total for the day

(3) *Breakfast* **Wok omelette:** heat a wok until hot and spray with low fat cooking spray. Add 2 sliced spring onions and fry for 1 minute. Add 1 beaten egg, 50 g (1³/₄ oz) cooked peas and a 30 g (1¹/₂ oz) slice of diced ham. Quickly swirl the wok, making the egg go up the sides of the pan (like a huge pancake), cook for 1–2 minutes, then roll up and serve. 1 small glass (100 ml/3¹/₂ fl oz) of grapefruit juice.

(4½) *Lunch* **Prawn sandwich:** spread 2 slices of medium bread with 1 tsp tomato ketchup mixed with 1 tbsp reduced fat mayonnaise and a squeeze of lemon juice. Fill with 60 g (2 oz) cooked peeled prawns and lots of wafer thin cucumber. Cut into quarters and serve.

(3½) *Dessert* **Fairy cakes:** cut a small circle of cake out of the top of a 15 g (¹/₂ oz) ready made fairy cake, cut in half and reserve. Fill the hole with ¹/₂ tsp crème fraîche and then 1 tsp Weight Watchers Apricot Fruit Spread. Decorate the top with the 2 reserved halves, like butterfly wings. A 60 g pot of low fat chocolate mousse.

(4½) *Dinner* **Hot and sour soup:** (see recipe) served with a 60 g (2 oz) vegetable spring roll.

(3½) **Y** *Dessert* **Fruit medley:** a 100 g pot of very low fat fruit fromage frais, 1 banana, 1 apple and 1 kiwi.

(1) *Snacks* Use 300 ml (10 fl oz) skimmed milk throughout the day.

Hot and sour soup

Takes 25 minutes *Serves 4*

11 POINTS *values per recipe*
220 calories *per serving*

1.2 litres (2 pints) chicken stock
350 g (12 oz) skinless boneless chicken breasts *sliced thinly*
75 g (2³/₄ oz) shiitake mushrooms *halved*
1 large red chilli *deseeded and sliced*
1 red or yellow pepper *deseeded and sliced*
1 large pak choi, about 150 g (5¹/₂ oz) *cut into quarters*
100 g (3¹/₂ oz) dried egg noodles
2 tablespoons Chinese cooking wine
3 tablespoons rice vinegar
2 tablespoons light soy sauce
1¹/₂ teaspoons white pepper
fresh coriander sprigs *to garnish*

1 Put the chicken stock into a large saucepan and bring to the boil. Add the chicken slices, bring back to the boil and simmer for 5 minutes.
2 Add the mushrooms, chilli and pepper and bring back to a simmer. Cook for 3 minutes. Then add the pak choi, egg noodles, cooking wine, rice vinegar, soy sauce and white pepper. Cook for a further 3 minutes until the chicken is cooked and the vegetables are tender.
3 Ladle into deep bowls, garnish with coriander and serve.

Y **Vegetarian tip:** use vegetable stock instead of chicken stock and replace the sliced chicken with the same quantity of sliced tofu, for a **POINTS** value of 2¹/₂ per serving.

Kebabs in a pitta

Takes 25 minutes to prepare, 20 minutes to cook *Serves 4*

❄ *kebabs only*

29 POINTS values per recipe

360 calories per serving

2 garlic cloves

2.5 cm (1 inch) fresh ginger *peeled and chopped*

1 x 25 g packet of fresh coriander

1 medium slice of white bread *torn into pieces*

400 g (14 oz) extra lean pork mince

1 egg *beaten*

4 spring onions *chopped finely*

1 red chilli *deseeded and chopped finely*

4 tablespoons reduced fat mayonnaise

To serve

4 x 60 g (2 oz) medium pitta breads *toasted*

a few salad leaves

1 sliced tomato

❶ Put 1 garlic clove, ginger and coriander into a food processor and whiz until finely chopped. Add the bread and whiz again until fine crumbs. Empty into a large bowl.

❷ Add the pork mince, egg, spring onions and chilli. Mix everything together (it's best to use your hands). Divide into eight portions and with wet hands, roll into eight sausages.

❸ Preheat the grill to medium hot. Thread each sausage carefully on to a metal skewer and grill for 15–20 minutes, turning until golden brown and cooked. Meanwhile, crush the remaining garlic and mix with the mayonnaise.

❹ Cut each pitta in half and place one sausage in each half with salad leaves, tomato slices and the garlic mayonnaise. Serve two halves per person.

Better than a takeaway

total for the

3½ ⓨ *Breakfast* **Crumpets:** 2 toasted crumpets spread with 1 tsp low fat polyunsaturated margarine and 2 tsp Weight Watchers Raspberry Fruit Spread. A peach.

5½ *Lunch* **Soup:** any soup with a **POINTS** value of 3 such as a 400 g can of Sainsbury's Minestrone, served with 2 crackerbreads spread with 2 tbsp reduced fat cottage cheese. 2 figs.

7 *Dinner* **Kebabs in a pitta:** (see recipe) served with a zero **POINTS** value salad.

1 ⓨ *Dessert* **Mango sorbet:** a 60 g (2 oz) scoop of mango sorbet served with 1 peeled and diced kiwi fruit.

3 *Snacks* Use 300 ml (10 fl oz) skimmed milk throughout the day. 300 ml (10 fl oz) chilled lager. A 100 g pot of very low fat plain fromage frais.

Lamb Provençal

Takes 30 minutes to prepare, 1 hour to cook *Serves 4*

13¹/₂ POINTS *values per recipe*

240 calories *per serving*

400 g (14 oz) lean lamb leg steak *cut into small chunks*

1 tablespoon plain flour

low fat cooking spray

1 onion *chopped finely*

1 garlic clove *sliced*

125 ml (4 fl oz) sweet sherry

600 ml (1 pint) lamb stock

400 g can of chopped tomatoes

1 tablespoon dried oregano

60 g (2 oz) black olives in brine *drained*

100 g (3¹/₂ oz) artichoke hearts in brine *drained and halved*

salt and freshly ground black pepper

fresh oregano *to garnish*

1 Dust the lamb in the flour. Heat a large lidded saucepan and spray with low fat cooking spray. Add the meat, in batches, and cook for 5 minutes, until brown on all sides. Remove and set aside.

2 Spray the pan with a little more low fat cooking spray and cook the onion and garlic for 3–4 minutes until softened. Add the sherry and bubble for a minute until slightly reduced.

3 Return the lamb to the saucepan and add the stock, chopped tomatoes and oregano. Bring to the boil, cover and simmer for 1 hour, stirring occasionally.

4 Season and stir through the olives and artichokes. Heat through for a couple of minutes then garnish with oregano and serve.

One pot wonder

total for the day

(4) Ⓨ *Breakfast* **Porridge:** a 30 g (1¹/₄ oz) bowl of porridge made with 150 ml (5 fl oz) skimmed milk. 1 toasted crumpet with marmite.

(6¹/₂) Ⓨ *Lunch* **Mushroom toasties:** microwave 50 g (1³/₄ oz) sliced mushrooms sprayed with low fat cooking spray for 1–2 minutes. Mix with 1 tbsp low fat soft garlic and herb cheese. Use to sandwich together 2 medium bread slices. Sprinkle over 25 g (1 oz) grated reduced fat Cheddar. Bake at 200°C for 15 minutes. A 150 g pot of low fat yogurt. 1 tube of Weight Watchers Fruities.

(4¹/₂) *Dinner* **Lamb Provençal:** (see recipe) served with 100 g (3¹/₂ oz) potato mashed with 1 tbsp skimmed milk, green beans, sugar snap peas and carrots.

(3¹/₂) Ⓨ *Dessert* **Raspberry dream:** stir 1 tbsp Tia Maria and ¹/₂ tsp orange zest into a 150 g pot of low fat plain yogurt. Serve with 100 g (3¹/₂ oz) raspberries and 2 squares (14 g) of chocolate grated over the top.

(1¹/₂) *Snacks* Use 150 ml (5 fl oz) skimmed milk throughout the day. A 210 g can of fruit cocktail in juice.

Chocolate dream

total for the day

(3½) 🅨 *Breakfast* **Frozen berry crush:** whiz a 150 g pot of low fat plain yogurt with 75 g (2³/₄ oz) frozen summer fruits and 3 tbsp skimmed milk. A 35 g medium slice of brown bread, toasted and spread with 2 tsp Weight Watchers Fruit Spread.

(4) *Lunch* **Panzanella salad:** in a bowl, mix together 50 g (1³/₄ oz) torn, cooked chicken, 25 g (1 oz) sliced mild pepperdew peppers, 10 torn basil leaves and a 40 g (1¹/₂ oz) medium slice of toasted and cubed ciabatta. Toss with a generous handful of salad leaves, halved cherry tomatoes, diced cucumber and 1 tbsp fat free Italian dressing. 1 tbsp reduced calorie coleslaw. A 210 g can of peaches in juice.

(6) *Dinner* **Tuna steak:** brush a 140 g (5 oz) tuna steak with 1 tsp sunflower oil and cook in a non stick frying pan or on a griddle pan for 5–8 minutes. Serve with 1 poached egg, green beans and 150 g (5¹/₂ oz) cooked, diced potatoes, sautéed with low fat cooking spray until golden.

(4) 🅨 *Dessert* **Chocolate torte:** (see recipe) served with 100 g (3¹/₂ oz) fresh raspberries.

(2½) *Snacks* Use 300 ml (10 fl oz) skimmed milk throughout the day. 1 light cream cracker and 1 tbsp low fat soft cheese.

Chocolate torte

Takes 15 minutes to prepare, 20 minutes to bake + 1 hour cooling

Serves 8

29 POINTS values per recipe

210 calories per serving

12 Weight Watchers Double Chocolate Cookies
40 g (1¹/₂ oz) low fat polyunsaturated margarine *melted*
3 eggs *separated*
75 g (2³/₄ oz) golden caster sugar
25 g (1 oz) cocoa
25 g (1 oz) plain flour
2 tablespoons chocolate spread
2 tablespoons low fat soft cheese

① Preheat the oven to Gas Mark 4/180°C/fan oven 160°C. Line a 19 cm (7¹/₂ inch) loose bottom round tin with non stick baking parchment. Whiz the chocolate cookies in a food processor to fine crumbs. Add the margarine and whiz again.

② Empty the crumbs into the prepared tin and using your fingers or knuckles press the crumbs evenly across the base to line. Set aside.

③ In a bowl, using an electric hand whisk, whisk the egg yolks and sugar until pale and fluffy. Then whisk in the cocoa and flour.

④ In another clean bowl, whisk the egg whites until soft peaks. Fold one third of the egg whites into the egg yolk mixture to loosen. Fold in the remaining egg whites until combined. Spoon into the tin and level the surface. Bake in the oven for 20 minutes. Remove from the oven and leave to cool for about 1 hour. (The cake will shrink down a little but don't worry.)

⑤ To make the chocolate frosting, gently warm the chocolate spread in a small saucepan and then mix in the soft cheese until smooth.

⑥ Remove the tin and the paper from the cake and transfer to a serving plate. Spread the chocolate frosting over the top, using a palette knife to swirl the frosting, if desired. Leave to set and then serve.

Black Forest trifle

Takes 20 minutes + 10 minutes cooling *Serves 4*

22¹/₂ POINTS *values per recipe*

325 calories *per serving*

1 x 500 g bag of frozen Black Forest fruits

1 tablespoon caster sugar

1 mulled wine spice bag

2 teaspoons cornflour mixed with 1 tablespoon water

4 Weight Watchers Chocolate Brownies *each cut into 9 cubes*

125 ml (4 fl oz) half fat crème fraîche

30 g (1¹/₄ oz) chilled plain chocolate

1 Put half the Black Forest fruits into a bowl and set aside. Put the remaining fruits into a small saucepan with 100 ml (3¹/₂ fl oz) water, sugar and mulled wine spice bag. Bring to the boil and rapidly boil for 5 minutes. Pass through a sieve into a jug, pressing the fruit with the back of a spoon to squeeze out all the juice. (You should have about 200 ml /7 fl oz juice).

2 Return the fruit juice to a small saucepan along with the dissolved cornflour. Bring to the boil and simmer for 1 minute, stirring until thickened. Pour this over the reserved frozen fruits in the bowl and leave to cool for 10 minutes.

3 Take four glasses and put three cubes of chocolate brownies into each glass. Top each glass with a spoonful of the fruit and sauce and then a dollop of half fat crème fraîche. Continue layering until everything is used up. Grate the chocolate over each and serve.

Go retro

4 *Breakfast* **Beans on toast:** heat 75 g (2³/₄ oz) cannellini beans with 1 tbsp half fat crème fraîche, 1 tbsp tomato purée, 1 tsp Worcestershire sauce and 1 tbsp water in a pan for 5 minutes. Season and serve on 1 medium slice (40 g/1¹/₂ oz) of toasted ciabatta.

3 *Lunch* **Pasta soup:** a can of ready made soup with a **POINTS** value of 2 such as a 26 g sachet of Weight Watchers from Heinz Broccoli and Cheddar Snack Soup with Tagliatelle. A 100 g pot of very low fat fruit fromage frais.

6 *Dinner* **Roasted vegetable polenta:** roast 75 g (2³/₄ oz) diced aubergine, 100 g (3¹/₂ oz) sliced courgette, ¹/₂ diced red pepper, 4 button mushrooms and 100 g (3¹/₂ oz) cubed ready made polenta for 40–45 minutes at 200°C. Toss with 1 tbsp pesto and top with watercress and sliced red onion.

5¹/₂ *Dessert* **Black Forest trifle:** (see recipe).

1¹/₂ *Snacks* Use 300 ml (10 fl oz) skimmed milk throughout the day. 1 apple.

Melon salad

Takes 30 minutes + 45 minutes cooling *Serves 2*

3¹/₂ POINTS *values per recipe*

100 calories *per serving*

2 tablespoons syrup from a jar of ginger

1 x 25 g packet of fresh mint leaves *stalks removed*

100 g (3¹/₂ oz) cantaloupe melon *peeled, deseeded and sliced into wedges*

100 g (3¹/₂ oz) honeydew melon *peeled, deseeded and sliced into wedges*

100 g (3¹/₂ oz) galia melon *peeled, deseeded and sliced into wedges*

1 x 15 g nugget of ginger in syrup *chopped*

a few fresh mint sprigs *to garnish*

1 Bring 150 ml (5 fl oz) water to the boil in a small saucepan and then add the ginger syrup. Boil rapidly boil for 10 minutes. Add the mint leaves and set aside for 30 minutes.

2 Pass the syrup through a sieve into a jug, pressing the mint leaves to squeeze out the juices. Put all the melon wedges into a large bowl and pour over the mint infusion. Leave for 15 minutes.

3 Divide the melon and mint infusion between bowls, scatter over the ginger and mint sprigs and serve.

Food to go

total for the day

3½ *Breakfast* A 150 g pot of low fat fruit yogurt. 1 peach and 1 nectarine.

5 *Lunch* **Picnic loaf:** cut the top off a 75 g (2³/₄ oz) roll. Scoop out most of the bread and then layer with 30 g (1¹/₄ oz) wafer thin ham, 4 basil leaves, 25 g (1 oz) sliced reduced fat mozzarella, 25 g (1 oz) drained and sliced roasted red pepper in brine and 25 g (1 oz) drained and sliced artichoke hearts in brine. Replace the top.

6½ *Dinner* **Juniper chicken:** bring 250 ml (9 fl oz) chicken stock, 250 ml (9 fl oz) white grape juice, a thyme sprig, 1 tbsp juniper berries to the boil. Add a 175 g (6 oz) skinless boneless chicken breast, simmer for 20 minutes. Stir in 2 tsp vegetable gravy granules and heat until thickened. Serve with broccoli, sliced marrow and 100 g (3¹/₂ oz) boiled potatoes.

2 *Dessert* **Melon salad:** (see recipe).

3 *Snacks* Use 300 ml (10 fl oz) skimmed milk throughout the day. A tube of Weight Watchers Fruities. 2 Jaffa Cakes.

Hot off the grill

(3½) **Y** *Breakfast* A 30 g (1¹/₄ oz) bowl of cereal with 150 ml (5 fl oz) skimmed milk and 1 banana.

(5½) *Lunch* **Turkey bagel:** spread 1 bagel with 2 tbsp low fat cottage cheese and top with a 30 g (1¹/₄ oz) slice of cooked turkey, 1 sliced spring onion and 2 sliced, sun dried tomatoes. 2 satsumas.

(5½) *Dinner* **Barbecued steak:** season a 125 g (4¹/₂ oz) beef rump steak with freshly ground black pepper and the zest of ¹/₂ a lemon. Spray with low fat cooking spray and barbecue (or grill) for 3–4 minutes, turn over and top with 25 g (1 oz) sliced reduced fat mozzarella. Barbecue (or grill) for 2–3 minutes until cooked to your liking and the mozzarella has melted. Serve with 125 g (4¹/₂ oz) barbecued corn on the cob and a large green salad.

(3) **Y** *Dessert* **Baked peaches:** (see recipe).

(2½) *Snacks* Use 150 ml (5 fl oz) skimmed milk throughout the day. 1 warmed Scotch pancake with 2 tsp golden syrup.

Baked peaches

Takes 10 minutes to prepare, 30 minutes to cook *Serves 4*

12 POINTS values per recipe

145 calories *per serving*

4 ripe peaches *halved and stoned*
4 tablespoons white wine
zest and juice of ¹/₂ an orange
1 tablespoon light brown sugar
2 teaspoons low fat polyunsaturated margarine
15 g (¹/₂ oz) amaretti biscuits *crushed*
4 tablespoons half fat crème fraîche

1 Preheat the oven to Gas Mark 6/200°C/fan oven 180°C.

2 Put the peach halves in an ovenproof dish, cut side up.

3 In a small jug, mix together the wine, orange zest and juice.

4 Pour over the peaches and sprinkle with the sugar. Dot with the margarine and bake in the oven for 25–30 minutes until golden and the juices have thickened.

5 Sprinkle over the crushed biscuits and serve with the crème fraîche.

Crêpes suzette

Takes 20 minutes *Serves 4*

10 POINTS *values per recipe*

235 calories *per serving*

50 g (1³/₄ oz) plain flour

a pinch of salt

1 egg

125 ml (4 fl oz) skimmed milk

low fat cooking spray

312 g can of mandarin orange segments in natural juice *drained and juice reserved*

2 tablespoons Weight Watchers Seville Orange Spread

1 orange *peeled and segmented*

a few fresh mint sprigs *to garnish*

4 tablespoons low fat plain yogurt *to serve*

1 Whisk together the flour, salt and egg in a bowl . Gradually whisk in the milk until the batter is smooth.

2 Heat a non stick frying pan and spray with low fat cooking spray. Spoon a ladleful of batter into the pan and swirl around to spread the mixture. Cook for 1–2 minutes, turning halfway until golden. Transfer to a plate. Repeat with the batter to make 3 more pancakes, spraying the frying pan with low fat cooking spray each time. Fold the pancakes into quarters and set aside.

3 Put the mandarin juice and orange spread into the frying pan and gently heat. Add the orange, mandarin segments and pancakes. Gently heat for 1–2 minutes until the pancakes have heated through and the juice has thickened. Garnish with mint sprigs and serve with the yogurt.

Pancake day

20 POINTS VALUE total for the day

3 *Breakfast* A 30 g (1¹/₄ oz) bowl of cereal with 150 ml (5 fl oz) skimmed milk. 100 g (3¹/₂ oz) bunch of grapes.

5 *Lunch* **Salami melt:** fill a 50 g (1³/₄ oz) bread roll with 1 salami slice and 1 sliced tomato. Top with 25 g (1 oz) sliced reduced fat mozzarella. Grill until melted.

7 *Dinner* **Creamy turkey lasagne:** cook ¹/₂ a finely chopped red onion and 50 g (1³/₄ oz) sliced mushrooms until soft. Add 125 g (4¹/₂ oz) lean turkey mince and brown. Stir in 1 tsp Garlic Italian seasoning and 25 g (1 oz) baby spinach. Stir to cook until wilted. Stir in 2 tbsp low fat soft cheese. Layer in a small ovenproof dish with 2 lasagne sheets and a small 200 g can of chopped tomatoes. Grate over 1 tbsp reduced fat Cheddar cheese. Bake at 200°C for 45 minutes. Serve with a green salad.

2¹/₂ *Dessert* **Crêpes suzette:** (see recipe).

2¹/₂ *Snacks* Use 300 ml (10 fl oz) skimmed milk throughout the day. 1 banana.

Lemon loaf

Takes 15 minutes to prepare, 30 minutes to cook + 10 minutes cooling *Serves 10*

 ✳

25 POINTS *values per recipe*

155 calories *per serving*

low fat cooking spray

200 g (7 oz) self raising flour

1 teaspoon bicarbonate of soda

zest of 2 lemons and the juice of 1 lemon

100 g (3^1/$_2$ oz) golden caster sugar

1 tablespoon poppy seeds

2 eggs *beaten*

50 g (1^3/$_4$ oz) low fat polyunsaturated margarine *melted*

4 tablespoons low fat plain yogurt

1 tablespoon icing sugar *sieved*

1 Preheat the oven to Gas Mark 4/180°C/fan oven 160°C. Spray a 1.2 litre (2 pints) loaf tin with low fat cooking spray and line with non stick baking parchment.

2 Put the flour, bicarbonate of soda, lemon zest, sugar and poppy seeds in a bowl.

3 Mix together in a jug the eggs, margarine and yogurt. Then stir into the flour mixture quickly (don't worry about any lumps). Spoon into the tin and level with the back of a spoon.

4 Bake in the oven on the middle shelf for 25–30 minutes until risen and it springs back when pressed. Remove from the oven and leave in the tin for 10 minutes. Mix together the lemon juice and icing sugar. Remove the cake from the tin, discard the paper and drizzle the icing over the cake to make a glaze.

A sweet ending

total for the day

(3^1/$_2$) *Breakfast* **Sausage roll:** grill 2 reduced fat pork sausages for 12–15 minutes until cooked. Spray a non stick frying pan with low fat cooking spray. Sauté 50 g (1^3/$_4$ oz) halved cherry tomatoes with 1 tbsp balsamic vinegar for 2–3 minutes. Serve the sausages in a 50 g (1^3/$_4$ oz) brown roll with the tomatoes.

(6^1/$_2$) *Lunch* **Turkey tortilla:** spread a flour tortilla wrap with 1 tbsp cranberry sauce, a 75 g (2^3/$_4$ oz) slice of cooked turkey and a handful of spinach. Roll up and serve. A 150 g pot of low fat plain yogurt. A 50 g packet of ready to eat semi dried apricots.

(5) *Dinner* **Jacket potato:** fill a 225 g (8 oz) jacket potato with 125 g (4^1/$_2$ oz) cooked, peeled prawns mixed with 2 tbsp low fat pineapple cottage cheese. Serve with a mixed salad, sliced pepper and grated carrot.

(2^1/$_2$) *Dessert* **Lemon loaf:** (see recipe).

(2^1/$_2$) *Snacks* Use 300 ml (10 fl oz) skimmed milk throughout the day. A 150 g (5^1/$_2$ oz) slice of cantaloupe melon, 1 kiwi and 100 g (3^1/$_2$ oz) grapes.

Index for
Core Plan

Index for *POINTS* Plan

Index by
POINTS values

6 POINTS values and under

apricot turnovers 50

baked egg buns 54

Black Forest trifle 84

creamy steak dauphinois 36

fruity couscous 53

primavera pasta 20

stir fried beef noodles 23

winter pork ragu 66

zesty seafood shells 32

7 POINTS values and under

chargrilled turkey steaks with korma rice 64

kebabs in a pitta 80

8 POINTS values and under

baked red pepper crumble 62

beef Wellington 76

9 POINTS values and under

baked chicken lentils 26

Index for the Core Plan Weekly *POINTS* allowance

If you're following the **Core Plan**, you have the flexibility to add non Core foods to your meals by using your optional weekly *POINTS* allowance of 21. You'll probably have noticed that the *POINTS* **Plan** recipes contain some **Core Plan** foods as ingredients; for example, in the Huntsman chicken on page 74, the only ingredients that are not on the **Core Plan** Food List are the brown sugar, tomato ketchup and the brown sauce. So, if you wanted to use the Huntsman chicken recipe, you would need to allocate $1/2$ *POINTS* value from your weekly *POINTS* allowance per serving.

With the help of this index you can easily use the *POINTS* **Plan** dishes in *menu plan eat enjoy* while following the **Core Plan**.

In the list opposite, you'll find the *POINTS* **Plan** recipes listed alphabetically, together with their page numbers and the number of weekly *POINTS* allowance each recipe, per serving, would use.

* Cornflakes and oats are used dry in this recipe and therefore are not on the **Core Plan** Food List.